Buzz Aldrin

Edward Asner

Neil and Lisa Beckerman

Ed Begley Jr.

Edward James Olmos

The Bellamy Brothers

esley Boone

The Bridges Family

Beau Br

rinkley

Erin Brockovich

Pierce and Keely Brosnan

Chef Leah Chase

Katie Couric

Ted Danson and Mary Steenburgen

Kristen Davis

Bruce Davison

Bo Derek

Hector Elizondo

Dennis Franz

Scott and Carol Glenn

Linda Gray

Steve Guttenberg

Edie Hand

Mariel Hemingway

Don Henley

Catherine Hicks

lizabeth Hurley

Kathy Ireland

Beverly Johnson

Senator Edward M. Kennedy

Graham Kerr

Swoosie Kurtz

Diane Ladd

Martin Landau

Jay Leno

Kenny Loggins

Joan Lunden

Pamela Sue Martin

Tim McGraw

Donna Mills

evin Nealon

Craig T. Nelson

Donny Osmond

Dolly Parton

Alexandra Paul

Chef Pepin

Bonnie Raitt

LeAnn Rimes

Wayne and Amy Rogers

Mickey and Jan Rooney

Martin Sheen

Kurtwood Smith

Senator Arlen Specter

Marlo Thomas

Lea Thompson

Cheryl Tiegs

John Travolta

Sela Ward

Dennis Weaver

Carnie and Wendy Wilson

Chef Martin Yan

Buzz Aldrin · Edward Asner · Neil and Lisa Beckerman

Ed Begley Jr. · Edward James Olmos · The Bellamy Brothers

Lesley Boone · The Bridges Family · Beau Bridges · Christie Brinkley

Erin Brockovich · Pierce and Keely Brosnan · Cheryl Chase

Chef Leah Chase · Katie Couric

Ted Danson and Mary Steenburgen · Kristen Davis · Bruce Davison

Bo Derek · Hector Elizondo · Dennis Franz

Scott and Carol Glenn · Linda Gray · Steve Guttenberg · Edie Hand

Mariel Hemingway · Don Henley · Catherine Hicks

Elizabeth Hurley · Kathy Ireland · Beverly Johnson · Senator Edward M. Kennedy

Graham Kerr · Swoosie Kurtz · Diane Ladd

Martin Landau · Jay Leno · Kenny Loggins · Joan Lunden

Pamela Sue Martin · Tim McGraw · Donna Mills

Kevin Nealon · Craig T. Nelson · Donny Osmond · Dolly Parton

Alexandra Paul · Chef Pepin · Bonnie Raitt

LeAnn Rimes · Wayne and Amy Rogers

Mickey and Jan Rooney · Martin Sheen · Kurtwood Smith

Senator Arlen Specter · Marlo Thomas · Lea Thompson · Cheryl Tiegs

John Travolta · Sela Ward · Dennis Weaver

Carnie and Wendy Wilson · Chef Martin Yan

Cooking Up An End

to

Childhood Hunger

in

AMERICA

....

Celebrity Cookbook

·

Acknowledgements

Cooking Up an End to Childhood Hunger in America was created to benefit Hunger Free America, a program
of the Entertainment Industry Foundation (EIF) founded by the EIF, the End Hunger Network and the Center
on Hunger and Poverty. Unilever Bestfoods is the founding sponsor of Hunger Free America.

We are grateful to everyone involved who shared their recipes and commentary with us and to the dedicated
teams and representatives from the Entertainment Industry Foundation, the End Hunger Network, Unilever Bestfoods,
Bragman Nyman Cafarelli, Cynthia Snyder PR, Hill & Knowlton PR, Guttman Associates, Lita Richardson Entertainment,
PMK, Rogers and Cowen, and Wolf Kasteller for their hard work and commitment to the success of this book.

Food photography by Colin Cooke, NY

Celebrity photography:
Edward Asner by Michael Greco, Christie Brinkley by © Timothy White 1998, Mariel Hemingway by Joseph Montezinos,
Kenny Loggins by Jay Blakesberg, Pamela Sue Martin and Scott & Carol Glenn by Peter Kredenser, Donny Osmond by
Andrew Eccles 2000, Dolly Parton by Dennis Carney B., Bonnie Raitt by Dana Tynan, LeAnn Rimes by Mark Liddell and
Rugrats™ Angelica by Nickelodeon®/Klasky Csupo.

Cooking Up An End

to

Childhood Hunger

in

AMERICA

·····························

Celebrity Cookbook

Unilever Bestfoods

End Hunger Network

Center on Hunger and Poverty

to benefit Hunger Free America, a program of the

Entertainment Industry Foundation

TABLE OF CONTENTS

Welcome to *Cooking Up An End to Childhood Hunger in America!* I hope you enjoy the wonderful, mouthwatering recipes in this book. I want to tell you a little about why we put this book together.

Many Americans don't realize there is a serious problem of hunger here in our own country. The purpose of this cookbook is to bring attention to this problem by gathering celebrities together to share their thoughts, as well as their recipes, with you.

Today 12 million children in America are not getting the food they need to grow and develop. Research has shown that even brief periods of hunger during a child's developing years can have a devastating impact on the individual, as well as on our society. Childhood hunger can permanently retard physical growth, brain development and cognitive functioning. It can lead to long-term emotional, medical and mental-health problems. Childhood hunger can also result in increased abuse of drugs and alcohol at early ages and increased rates of incarceration.

Cooking Up An End to Childhood Hunger in America is a project of Hunger Free America, a program of the Entertainment Industry Foundation. For 60 years, the Entertainment Industry Foundation has brought together the collective power of the entertainment industry to address the most critical issues of our time. Through the Hunger Free America program, the Entertainment Industry Foundation joins Unilever Bestfoods, the End Hunger Network, the Center on Hunger and Poverty, and Children Uniting Nations to take on the challenge of ending childhood hunger. Ending hunger is not a mystery; by building on such successful federal and state interventions as the school breakfast and lunch programs, childhood hunger can be eliminated.

Thank you for your participation by purchasing this book. Throughout its pages you will find important information to help end hunger in your community. My hope is that you will continue to be involved for as long as it takes to end childhood hunger in America.

{ Fact: One of every six children in America lives in poverty, and one-third of all U.S. children born today will live in poverty before they reach the age of sixteen. }

All of us who have participated in *Cooking Up An End to Childhood Hunger in America* are committed to raising the awareness and funds necessary to bring an end to this devastating crisis. I thank everyone involved for sharing their favorite recipes, as well as their hopes for a future without hunger.

Finally, I want to extend a very special thanks to Unilever Bestfoods, which is providing corporate support to Hunger Free America. Unilever Bestfoods has also underwritten the costs to produce this cookbook and lent its kitchens to taste-test each recipe.

Please enjoy these wonderful dishes with your family and friends. Everyone in America should have a place at the table to enjoy its bounty.

JEFF BRIDGES

CHAIRMAN
HUNGER FREE AMERICA, A PROGRAM OF THE
ENTERTAINMENT INDUSTRY FOUNDATION

FOUNDER
END HUNGER NETWORK

{ Fact: Undernutrition and other factors associated with poverty can permanently impair brain function. }

Hunger is about pain and deprivation—the pain of a child who quietly suffers another day with an empty stomach, the anguish of a mother who is unable to feed her child, the despair of a family that must choose between going without meals or paying the rent.

You may not know anyone who has suffered from hunger. Perhaps you think hunger is limited to the homeless whom we see each day begging on the streets. But hunger goes much deeper—into a hidden America where working families live at the poverty level, unable to provide adequate nourishment for their children.

As campaign chair of Hunger Free America, it is my mission to involve our community in the solution to this problem. Be aware! We desperately need your help in bringing about change and ending this tragedy. Please send us your expressions of concern. Your statements may become part of our message through the media, which I will also deliver to President and Mrs. Bush and to other key leaders of our country. Let your voices be heard!
Visit www.hungerfreeamerica.org.

BO DEREK
CAMPAIGN CHAIR
HUNGER FREE AMERICA

{ Fact: Twelve million children live in food insecure homes, where food may be
scarce or diets altered due to limited incomes. }

As a major food company, Unilever Bestfoods is honored to be a part of *Cooking Up An End to Childhood Hunger in America*. We are devoted to helping the more than 30 million Americans who go hungry every day—tragically, almost half are children. Because we believe every child should have the opportunity to grow up healthy to reach his or her maximum potential, we are committed to working with the Entertainment Industry Foundation, through its Hunger Free America program, and the End Hunger Network to help put an end to hunger in America.

As the maker of such familiar brands as Lipton® tea, Hellmann's® mayonnaise, Ragú® pasta sauce, Shedd's Spread Country Crock®, Wish-Bone® salad dressings, and Skippy® peanut butter, Unilever Bestfoods has a long history of supporting Hunger Free America. Each year, we donate more than $10 million worth of products through the nation's food banks. Now not only are we continuing this tradition, but we are also significantly stepping up our support by donating $3 million in cash plus an additional $3 million in the form of strong marketing support. In fact, we are rallying the grocery trade's support by creating customized programs with many stores. Many of the nation's largest food retailers are participating. With the expansion of programs like these, we can hope to raise upward of $20 million over the next five years to help end hunger in America.

NEIL BECKERMAN
PRESIDENT & CEO
UNILEVER BESTFOODS NORTH AMERICA

{ Fact: Sixty percent of people who receive emergency food assistance
are children and their parents. }

———

When 30 million Americans face hunger, we are all at risk. As a country, we value family, education and independence. Hunger is an enemy to all three. Our society will not develop community, grow spiritually or continue to prosper materially unless we accept the challenge to end childhood hunger.

MICHAEL ROBITAILLE, EXECUTIVE DIRECTOR
END HUNGER NETWORK

None of the other industrialized countries still puts up with widespread hunger, and we certainly don't have to allow millions of children to go hungry in the United States. From a religious perspective, the feasibility of ending widespread hunger is a blessing and responsibility from God.

REVEREND DAVID BECKMANN
PRESIDENT, BREAD FOR THE WORLD

Some 12 million children live in households that know the pain of hunger or the uncertainty of their next meal. Even mild undernutrition, like missing meals here and there due to not having enough food in the house, robs children of their natural potential. Hungry children suffer from impaired cognitive functioning, and for many of them, the result will be permanent disability. Of all the problems that afflict our people, hunger is the most solvable. The expansion of child nutrition programs in the states will ensure that they are there for all who are at risk.

DR. J. LARRY BROWN
CENTER ON HUNGER AND POVERTY

Our Lord commands us to feed the hungry—yet nearly 800 million people in the world, 200 million of them children, go hungry. In the United States, 30 million people live in households that experience or are at risk of hunger. The scandal of world hunger stands as a challenge to all its inhabitants, but especially to those of us who claim as our own the values of the Gospel, and to those of us living in prosperous societies. We must continue and increase our efforts to assist our hungry brothers and sisters, acting as individuals, as nations and as the People of God. As you prepare the meals provided in this volume, I invite you to begin with a prayer of gratitude for the blessings God has bestowed upon you, and of petition asking God to show you how you can help to feed His hungry children.

HIS EMINENCE CARDINAL ROGER MAHONEY
ARCHBISHOP OF LOS ANGELES
CHAIRMAN, DOMESTIC POLICY COMMITTEE OF THE UNITED STATES CONFERENCE OF CATHOLIC BISHOPS

{ Fact: Single mothers with children registered the highest level of food stress. Nearly 30 percent of households in this group were food insecure, and 8 percent were food insecure with hunger. }

The American Dietetic Association considers access to nutritious food to be a fundamental human right. ADA supports Hunger Free America's efforts to raise national awareness of hunger in this country. Through coordinated, aggressive action—by government and the private sector—we can end hunger and achieve food and nutrition security for everyone.

AMERICAN DIETETIC ASSOCIATION

There is so much potential in our children, our future. Each generation has the ability to create a new society. If we continue to inflict suffering and intolerance upon our children, the world will continue its increase in violence and despair. We have the ability to break the cycle now and create compassionate and loving children of the future.

DAPHNA EDWARDS ZIMAN, FOUNDER
CHILDREN UNITING NATIONS

Food is a fundamental building block of a healthy life and a healthy society. Hunger interferes with brain development, cognitive functioning, behavior and a child's ability to learn, grow and form relationships. The result: lost brainpower, lost hope for a better future and lost productivity for our nation. Federal and state governments are a major line of defense against hunger through their food assistance programs—a cornerstone of our national recipe to eradicate hunger. Hunger is a public health problem and demands action from every part of our society. That's why we must continue to work together across the public and private sectors so that we can soon reach the time when children have to turn to the history books to learn there was a threat to their health called hunger.

REAR ADMIRAL SUSAN J. BLUMENTHAL, M.D.
U.S. ASSISTANT SURGEON GENERAL

It is a scandal that, in a land of such abundance, millions of children still know the pain of hunger. There's no better way to fulfill Judaism's mandate to "repair the world" than by making a difference in the lives of hungry children. Among the essential efforts to end childhood hunger in America, we need to support the school lunch and food stamp programs.

RABBI ARNOLD RACHLIS
MAZON: A JEWISH RESPONSE TO HUNGER

{ Fact: Hunger may result in malnutrition. But often food insecurity and hunger occur without the visible signs of stark malnutrition typically associated with impoverished nations. }

An American Tragedy

More than 30 million people in America are unsure from where their next meal will come. This type of nutritional deprivation is called food insecurity and often leads to hunger. When people experience hunger, the physical pain they feel is very different from the pangs the rest of us get when it's simply time for our next meal. While hunger here takes different forms than in the Third World, it still takes a serious toll, especially on the bodies and minds of our young children.

THE IMPACT ON KIDS

In an undernourished state (even missing a meal or two), a young child's mind does not function normally. This condition often leads to permanent cognitive impairments. Hunger also interferes with normal development, sometimes stopping height and weight gain altogether.

IN SHORT, HUNGER CAN:

- Limit growth. The Centers for Disease Control and Prevention reports that 9.7 percent of low-income children under 2 years were of short stature in 1997. This rate is twice as high as normally expected.
- Impair brain development.
- Reduce immune function so that a poorly nourished child is more likely to become ill and miss school.
- Cause iron deficiency, which lowers the immune response and a child's ability to learn in school.
- Limit a child's cognitive development, overall learning potential and productive capacity as an adult.

Researchers also have reported that hungry children demonstrate higher levels of irritable and aggressive behaviors than those who are not hungry.

THE CHILDREN BEHIND THE STATISTICS

Besides long-term physical consequences, hunger has devastating emotional effects as well. Many of us are unaware of them, however, because the smallest sufferers often remain silent.

{ Fact: The longer a child's nutritional, emotional and educational needs go unmet, the greater the likelihood of permanent impairment of cognitive function. }

ROBERT'S STORY:
"IT'S NOT MY TURN"

Six-year-old Robert and his three brothers live with their parents in a small house at the edge of town in Northern Idaho. His father works as a logger and his mother is unemployed. Robert attends the local Head Start program. He is a quiet, shy boy who mostly plays by himself. The director of the program, Susan Wilson, tried on many occasions to get closer to Robert.

One day, Robert seemed to be more withdrawn than usual. Susan asked what was wrong. After some coaxing, Robert answered, "I'm very hungry."

"Didn't you eat your breakfast at home?" she asked.

"It's not my turn," Robert whispered.

"What do you mean? Not your turn?"

"Today, it's not my turn to eat," he replied.

To cope with the shortage of food, each member of Robert's family goes without eating one or two meals each week. This painful solution to the problem is not as rare as you might believe. Families living in poverty must pay for such necessities as gasoline, electricity and rent too. The budget for food is reduced to make limited funds cover household expenses.

ANNA'S STORY:
"ICE MAKES THE PAIN GO AWAY"

Eleven-year-old Anna lives in North Carolina. Even though her mother works full time, there often is not enough money left for food after she pays the rent and other bills. Both she and Anna frequently miss dinner, and even though Anna tries to fill up on her school lunch, it usually does not tide her over until bedtime. To cover up the pain of an empty stomach so she can sleep, Anna chews on ice cubes. "Even though it's not really food," she reports, "the ice tricks my stomach into thinking that it's full."

BABY CARL'S STORY:
"IT SHOULDN'T HURT TO BE A MOTHER"

Christine is the mother of Carl, a blue-eyed baby of 14 months. Little Carl's father broke his back on a construction project and is now permanently disabled. The family relies on emergency food donations, but often their cupboard is bare. Christine knows the value of good nutrition but due to their family circumstances,

{ Fact: Children in low-income families usually consume insufficient calories, and families often cope with limited food dollars by purchasing foods that are less expensive but higher in fat. }

Baby Carl's pediatrician found that he had dropped dangerously low on height and weight charts. Carl was placed in a special "growth-failure clinic" at a local hospital. While he's responding to the nutritional supplementation he gets there, Christine is worried about how she will care for him once he is able to come back home. "I try to do everything I can for him," Christine says, but she frets that it won't be enough. "It shouldn't have to hurt like this to be a mother."

PATRICIA'S STORY:
"STRETCHING THE BABY'S FORMULA"

"My name is Denise and I am 23 years old. I live in Chicago with my 4-year-old son, Hunter, and my 18-month-old daughter, Patricia. I share an apartment with my sister. My ex-husband seldom pays child support so I am the sole provider for my son, my daughter and myself. I work at a fast food restaurant for $7.50 an hour, but I am taking some college courses and I want to get a better job.

"Things are really hard. After I pay for child care, my rent and utilities and the bus pass, I only have $250 left for food for the month. I can sometimes get food at my church, but not always. When money is really short, I have to stretch things—like I'll add water to my baby's formula. I don't want to, but she needs to have her stomach full or she cries a lot. I really feel bad, but I don't know what else to do."

WHAT'S ALREADY BEING DONE

During the 1960s and 1970s, our nation's leaders nearly ended hunger by working together on a bipartisan basis to create and expand federal nutrition programs, which research has found to be very effective when fully utilized. The current programs are:

THE FOOD STAMP PROGRAM: The fundamental mission of the program is to help low-income people buy food. To qualify to receive food stamps, households must have a gross income below the official poverty level, and have few assets, such as cars. The program is highly effective but needs to be expanded. Studies have found that bureaucratic obstacles prevent up to a quarter of eligible households from receiving the coverage to which they are entitled, and funding cuts have placed more poor families at risk.

{ Fact: Poor children who attend school hungry perform below nonhungry, low-income peers on standardized test scores. }

THE SCHOOL LUNCH PROGRAM: Authorized by the Child Nutrition Act of 1946 to "safeguard the health and well-being of the nation's children," this federally funded program provides free or reduced-price nutritious lunches to qualifying children at participating schools and residential child-care institutions. Studies show that low-income children depend on the program for one-third to one-half of their nutritional intake each day.

THE SCHOOL BREAKFAST PROGRAM: This federally funded program provides free or reduced-price morning meals to qualifying children at participating schools and residential child-care institutions. But many children who qualify still go hungry because many school districts do not offer it.

THE SUMMER FOOD PROGRAM: This program provides meals to low-income children in the summer months. However, there are not enough summer food programs operating where eligible children live, so only about 20 percent of kids who participate in the School Lunch Program also receive summer meals.

THE SUPPLEMENTAL FOOD PROGRAM FOR WOMEN, INFANTS AND CHILDREN (WIC): Designed to safeguard the health of pregnant, postpartum and breast-feeding women, infants and children under 5 years of age. Household income must be no more than 185 percent of the poverty level, and participants must be at nutritional risk, based on abnormal weight gain during pregnancy, iron-deficiency anemia or related health risks. A General Accounting Office study concluded that for every dollar spent on WIC, $3.50 is saved by averting medical and other related expenditures.

BUT IT'S NOT ENOUGH

Unfortunately, these federal programs often fall short. To help remedy this, an array of emergency food programs have sprung up around the nation. Largest among them are food banks, which receive, store and distribute food products donated by manufacturers and grocery chains. The largest food bank system, America's Second Harvest, is a network of nearly 200 programs covering all states.

Food banks distribute their products to local programs. Nearly 50,000 agencies, such as churches and social service agencies, offer bags of groceries to needy families through this system, although most of them report that they often run out of food. Many communities also have soup kitchens where hungry people can go for a meal. While these facilities used to serve mainly single adults, their largest growing segment of clients is families with children.

{ Fact: Supplemental feeding programs help to offset the threats that inadequate nutrition pose to a child's capacity to learn and perform in school. }

We can be proud of all the current work being done to alleviate hunger. But it's a temporary solution at best. The people who work in these programs say that they have a job that should not exist. No one should go hungry in a wealthy nation. Our goals are to strengthen our most effective state and national programs that prevent hunger, so that parents do not have to take their children to a soup kitchen in order to get an emergency handout.

WHAT CAN YOU DO?

Hunger in America is such an overwhelming problem that it may seem there's nothing any individual can do to make much difference. But that's simply not true. Every adult (and child) can make a real contribution to ending this tragedy once and for all. Here's how:

1. Contribute to hunger organizations in your community. Your gifts of money or time can make a real difference, both in the quantity and quality of the assistance that can be provided. Remember that more than half of all people requesting emergency assistance are members of families with children.

2. Learn more about hunger in your community and state. If you volunteer at a local food bank or food pantry operated by your church, synagogue or mosque, you will be astounded to discover who is going hungry. You can also learn more about the hunger problem by visiting the Hunger Free America Website (*http://www.hungerfreeamerica.org*) and by contacting your local Hunger Free America state coalition leaders (see page 142 for state-by-state listings). Through them you will discover the specific hunger problems facing your state. You can also broaden your awareness of the problems and the solutions that can end hunger.

3. Advocate for ending hunger in your community, state and country. The enormity of the problem of hunger requires both national and local intervention. Hungry children do not have any political power. They cannot affect the outcome of an election or contribute to political campaigns. If you believe that childhood hunger should be eradicated, you must communicate this to your elected officials. The Hunger Free America Website includes a special section enabling you to e-mail your national and local political representatives. Let them know how you feel about ending hunger and your voice will be heard.

{
Fact: The fastest growing segment of the hungry is single mothers and their children.
Nearly 30 percent of single-parent households are food insecure. Children of low-income families usually
consume insufficient calories. In addition, about 25 percent of poor children in the U.S. experience
iron deficiency, which is associated with impaired brain development.
}

Cooking Up An End

to

Childhood Hunger

in

AMERICA

···

Celebrity Cookbook

◆

{ RECIPES }

Word history as in Scholastic Dictionary:
Recipe came from the Latin word *recipere* meaning *to receive*. First used by doctors who wrote it at the top of instructions
for making medicines. The word later also came to apply to instructions for making food.

"If we can conquer space, we can conquer childhood hunger.
Americans have accomplished such wondrous feats. The space program
began with a commitment, which enabled us to overcome
the myriad obstacles that stood in our way.
Surely, we can and must eliminate this earthly catastrophe.
It all begins with a commitment."

BUZZ ALDRIN

PREPARATION TIME: 10 MINUTES

COOK TIME: 45 MINUTES

....

2 teaspoons olive oil (Bertolli®)

2½- to 3-pound chicken, cut into serving pieces

2 large cloves garlic, finely chopped

⅓ cup pitted kalamata olives or pitted ripe olives, halved

2 teaspoons chopped fresh rosemary, or 1 teaspoon dried rosemary leaves, crushed

½ cup orange juice

3¼ cups (one 26-ounce jar) marinara sauce (Ragú® Old World Style®)

½ teaspoon grated orange peel

¼ teaspoon ground black pepper

Rosemary sprigs, for garnish

1. In a 12-inch skillet, heat oil over medium-high heat and brown chicken. Remove chicken and set aside; reserve drippings.

2. Add garlic, olives and rosemary to reserved drippings and cook over medium heat, stirring occasionally, 2 minutes. Add orange juice, stirring up brown bits from bottom of skillet.

3. Stir in marinara sauce, orange peel and pepper. Bring to a boil over high heat. Return chicken to skillet. Reduce heat to low and simmer, covered, 35 minutes, or until chicken is no longer pink. Garnish with rosemary.

Makes 4 servings

Serving suggestion: Serve over hot rice.

"There are genuinely sufficient
resources in the world to ensure that no one, nowhere,
at no time should go hungry."

EDWARD ASNER

MEDITERRANEAN STEW

PREPARATION TIME: 20 MINUTES
COOK TIME: 2 HOURS, 20 MINUTES
CHILL TIME: OVERNIGHT

....

1 pound chuck steak, cut into ½-inch cubes
1 pound sweet Italian sausage
1½ cups burgundy or dry red wine
1 can (6 ounces) tomato paste
2 teaspoons paprika
1 teaspoon salt
¾ teaspoon black pepper
3 garlic cloves, finely chopped
1 pound cooked ham, cut into 1-inch cubes
3 medium onions, coarsely chopped
1 medium red bell pepper, coarsely chopped
2 cans (16 ounces each) garbanzo beans (chickpeas), rinsed and drained
¼ cup chopped fresh parsley
1 teaspoon grated lemon peel
1 head green cabbage, cut into wedges

1. In a Dutch oven or heavy saucepot, brown beef and sausage; drain.

2. Slice sausage and return to Dutch oven. Stir in 2 cups water, wine, tomato paste, paprika, salt, pepper and garlic. Bring to a boil over high heat. Reduce heat and simmer, covered, stirring occasionally, 1½ hours, or until meat is tender.

3. Stir in all remaining ingredients except cabbage. Simmer, covered, 20 minutes, stirring occasionally.

4. Stir in cabbage and simmer, stirring occasionally, until cabbage is crisp-tender, about 15 minutes.

5. Cover and chill in refrigerator overnight to develop flavors.

6. Skim fat from surface of stew and reheat in microwave or on stovetop.

Makes 8 servings

Serving suggestion: Tall glasses of Lipton® Iced Tea go well with this flavorful dish.

"Putting an end to hunger is not only an initiative we support in the corporate arena, but also a personal one. As the parents of two, it shocks us to think that every night 12 million children go to bed hungry. We can only imagine how horrible it must be to have to choose between paying the gas bill or feeding your family. No one should have to face that choice. We are truly dedicated to this cause and sincerely appreciate your support of this cookbook. Wishing you health and happiness,"

NEIL AND LISA BECKERMAN

(NEIL IS THE PRESIDENT & CEO, UNILEVER BESTFOODS NORTH AMERICA)

PREPARATION TIME: 5 MINUTES

COOK TIME: 20 MINUTES

....

1 can (14 ounces) artichoke hearts, drained and chopped

1 cup mayonnaise (Hellmann's® or Best Foods®)

1 cup (about 4 ounces) grated Parmesan cheese

1 clove garlic, minced (optional)

1 can chopped green chilies (optional)

1. Preheat oven to 350°F. In a 1-quart casserole, combine all ingredients.

2. Bake, uncovered, 20 minutes, or until heated through.

3. Serve with crackers or tortilla chips.

Makes 2½ cups

"We, who have so much, must do more to help
those in need. And most of all, we must live simply, so that
others may simply live."

ED BEGLEY JR.

"We must come to terms with our responsibility to be the gatekeepers
to end childhood hunger. Our love for life can propel us to share and provide
a secure future for the children of our country."

EDWARD JAMES OLMOS

PREPARATION TIME: 5 MINUTES
COOK TIME: 15 MINUTES

1 pound asparagus, tough stem ends removed

4 teaspoons fresh lemon juice

2 teaspoons extra-virgin olive oil (Bertolli®)

2 teaspoons orange juice

Cayenne pepper, to taste

Salt and black pepper, to taste

1. Cut asparagus into 3-inch pieces; steam until crisp-tender. Set aside.

2. Meanwhile, in small bowl, blend lemon juice, olive oil, orange juice, cayenne pepper, salt and black pepper.

3. To serve, arrange asparagus on platter, then drizzle with dressing.

Makes 4 servings

Serving suggestion: Serve with Roasted Chicken Au Jus. To make 4 servings, preheat oven to 425°F. Stir 1 envelope Lipton® Recipe Secrets® Onion Soup Mix and 2 tablespoons Bertolli® Olive Oil together until well combined. Arrange 2½ pounds bone-in chicken pieces in broiler pan with rack removed; brush with oil mixture. Bake, basting occasionally, 40 minutes, or until chicken is no longer pink. Transfer chicken to serving platter. To create a gravy, add ½ cup hot water to pan and stir, scraping brown bits from bottom. Serve over chicken.

"We are always happy to be involved with a program to end hunger. In a society where we have so much and so many things go to waste, we sometimes don't realize that there are many people in the world who go without food. Hopefully, our small contribution will help feed someone somewhere, because that is how it starts."

THE BELLAMY BROTHERS

PREPARATION TIME: 10 MINUTES

STAND TIME: 1 HOUR

COOK TIME: 1 HOUR, 50 MINUTES

....

1 bag (16 ounces) pinto beans

1 tablespoon olive oil (Bertolli®)

1 pound ground sirloin beef

1 medium onion, chopped

2 tablespoons chili powder

2 medium cloves garlic, finely chopped

3¼ cups (26-ounce jar) chunky garden-style pasta sauce (Ragú®)

3 jalapeño peppers, finely chopped

1½ teaspoons salt

4 ounces shredded cheddar cheese, for garnish

1. In a large stockpot, cover beans with water. Bring to a boil over high heat and boil 2 minutes. Remove from heat and let stand, covered, 1 hour.

2. Return stockpot to heat and bring to a boil. Reduce heat and simmer, covered, 1½ hours, or until beans are tender. Drain, reserving 1 cup liquid.

3. Meanwhile, in a 4-quart saucepan, heat oil and brown ground beef with onion, chili powder and garlic about 5 minutes; drain.

4. Stir in pasta sauce, cooked beans, reserved bean liquid, jalapeño peppers and salt. Simmer, covered, 10 minutes, or until heated through, stirring occasionally. Garnish with cheese and serve.

Makes 4 servings

Serving suggestion: Accompany this hearty dish with some warm cornbread.

"We are a country that prides itself on power and wealth, yet there are millions of children who go hungry every day. It is our responsibility not only as a nation, but as individuals, to get involved. So next time you pass someone on the street who is in need, remember how lucky you are, and don't turn away."

LESLEY BOONE

MINI ZUCCHINI PIZZAS

PREPARATION TIME: 10 MINUTES
COOK TIME: 16 MINUTES

....

1 tablespoon olive oil (Bertolli®)

1 small zucchini, thinly sliced

½ cup chopped green onions (scallions)

6 English muffins, halved and toasted

1⅔ cups (14-ounce jar) pizza sauce (Ragú®)

2 tablespoons grated Parmesan cheese

1 cup shredded Muenster or mozzarella cheese (about 4 ounces)

1. Preheat oven to 400°F. In a 12-inch skillet, heat oil over medium-high heat and cook zucchini and green onions 5 minutes, or until tender; set aside.

2. On ungreased baking sheet, arrange muffin halves. Evenly spread sauce on each half, then top with vegetable mixture and remaining ingredients. Bake 10 minutes, or until cheese is melted.

Makes 6 servings

THE BRIDGES FAMILY

"It has always distressed me to know that as we enjoy
the bounty of our own food, there are too many others who do not have
enough to sustain themselves or their families.
Thank God that there are those among us who care enough to work
on the concept that NO ONE in this rich country of
ours need ever go hungry."

DOROTHY BRIDGES

PREPARATION TIME: 25 MINUTES
CHILL TIME: UP TO 24 HOURS

4 cups shredded iceberg lettuce
⅔ cup chopped fresh parsley
1 red or green bell pepper, coarsely chopped
2 cups coarsely chopped cauliflower or broccoli
3 stalks celery, thinly sliced
2 large carrots, shredded
2 large zucchini, shredded
1 package (10 ounces) frozen green peas, thawed
1 cup mayonnaise (Hellmann's® or Best Foods®)
1 cup sour cream
2 tablespoons Dijon mustard
2 teaspoons garlic salt (Lawry's®)
1 teaspoon dried basil leaves
1 teaspoon dried rosemary, crumbled
1 tablespoon fresh oregano, or 1 teaspoon dried oregano leaves
½ teaspoon black pepper
2 cups shredded cheddar cheese (about 8 ounces)
½ cup thinly sliced green onions (scallions)
½ pound bacon, crisp-cooked and crumbled

1. In a 5- to 6-quart serving dish, arrange lettuce on bottom. Evenly layer parsley, red pepper, cauliflower, celery, carrots, zucchini and peas on top of lettuce.
2. In small bowl, combine mayonnaise, sour cream, mustard, garlic salt, basil, rosemary, oregano and pepper; spread evenly over top.
3. Sprinkle with cheese and green onions. Cover and chill in refrigerator up to 24 hours.
4. Garnish with bacon and serve.

Makes 12 servings

"Childhood hunger is a hidden tragedy. In cities and towns across
our country, millions of children are quietly going without the food they need
to grow and develop. They don't share their problem
with friends or teachers because of the terrible shame they feel. When we
work to end childhood hunger, we are giving our love to kids
who need it so much but will never ask for it."

BEAU BRIDGES

BEAU'S FAVORITE HOT FUDGE SUNDAE SAUCE

PREPARATION TIME: 5 MINUTES

COOK TIME: 7 MINUTES

....

1 cup sugar

2 squares (1 ounce each) unsweetened chocolate, chopped

¾ cup milk

1 teaspoon vanilla extract

¼ cup butter or margarine (I Can't Believe It's Not Butter!® Spread)

1. In small saucepan, bring sugar, chocolate and milk to a boil over medium-high heat. Cook, stirring frequently, 5 minutes.

2. Remove from heat; stir in vanilla and butter or margarine until melted.

3. In medium bowl, with electric mixer at medium speed, beat chocolate mixture until thickened, about 2 minutes. Serve immediately.

Makes 1⅓ cups sauce

Recipe provided by Beau's mom, Dorothy Bridges

Serving suggestion: Generously spoon over Breyers® Natural Strawberry Ice Cream.

"America and Americans always rise to the occasion.
If we say we are going to stamp out hunger, I believe we will.
Thanks, End Hunger Network, for the opportunity to help."

CHRISTIE BRINKLEY

TUNA SALAD SPLASH

PREPARATION TIME: 20 MINUTES

....

2 cans (12 ounces each) chunk light tuna in water, drained

1 large cucumber, peeled, seeded and diced

3 stalks celery, chopped

3 endive, chopped

1 package (8 ounces) edamame (precooked soybeans), shelled

1 bunch arugula, chopped

½ teaspoon kosher salt or sea salt

¼ teaspoon lemon pepper (Lawry's®)

1 teaspoon finely chopped garlic

1½ teaspoons chopped fresh basil, thyme, tarragon and/or sage

½ cup Oriental orange dressing (Hellmann's® or Best Foods®)

Boston, Bibb or other lettuce leaves

1. In large bowl, combine all ingredients except lettuce leaves; mix well.

2. Divide lettuce leaves among 4 plates and top with tuna salad.

Makes 4 servings

Recipe created by Joan Kenley

Serving suggestion: Pour some Lipton® Soup Secrets® Noodle Soup into mugs for a satisfying accompaniment.

"Few Americans really know anything about hunger in this country
or about who suffers from this cruel affliction. I do know!
I was formerly a member of that little-known, leading statistical group:
Single Working Mothers With Children. Most of our citizenry
believes that hunger only affects people who are lazy or people who are just
looking for a handout, people who don't want to work, but, sadly,
that is not true. Over one-third of our hungry people are
innocent children who are members of households that simply cannot
provide enough food or proper nutrition. And to think of
the elderly suffering from malnutrition is just too hard for most of us.
Unlike Third World nations, in our country, the problem is not
having too little—it is about caring enough!
Write your senators and promote support for the hungry!"

ERIN BROCKOVICH

PREPARATION TIME: 20 MINUTES

COOK TIME: 15 MINUTES

....

8 ounces angel hair pasta, cooked and drained

¾ cup Oriental orange dressing (Hellmann's® or Best Foods®), divided

¼ cup sliced green onions (scallions)

¼ cup chopped fresh cilantro (coriander), plus more for garnish

⅓ cup chopped salted peanuts

4 salmon fillets (about 6 ounces each)

Salt and ground black pepper, to taste

1. In large bowl, toss hot pasta with ½ cup dressing, green onions, cilantro and peanuts. Return to pot and cover to keep warm.

2. Meanwhile, grill or broil salmon and season, if desired, with salt and ground black pepper.

3. To serve, divide pasta mixture among 4 bowls, then top with salmon. Drizzle with the remaining ¼ cup dressing. Garnish, if desired, with additional fresh cilantro.

Makes 4 servings

Recipe created by chefs Mary Corpening Barber and Sara Corpening Whiteford

Serving suggestion: Tall glasses of Minty Green Tea Lemonade go well with this dish. To make 8 servings, bring 4 cups water to a boil and pour over 6 Lipton® Green Tea bags. Cover and brew 2 minutes. Remove tea bags and let cool. In 2-quart pitcher, combine cooled tea with 1 can (12 ounces) frozen lemonade concentrate, ½ cup fresh mint leaves and 2½ cups cold water. Chill at least 2 hours. Strain, if desired. Serve in ice-filled glasses and garnish, if desired, with lemon wedges.

"Many people may think that hunger is unavoidable
in any society, even a society that is blessed with great abundance. That is not
true. The European community does not have widespread
hunger. America, which leads the world in so many ways, can end
childhood hunger within its borders."

PIERCE AND KEELY BROSNAN

PREPARATION TIME: 10 MINUTES

CHILL TIME: 3 HOURS TO OVERNIGHT

....

1 cup mayonnaise (Hellmann's® or Best Foods®)

1 cup sour cream

⅓ cup crumbled Maytag blue cheese (about 1½ ounces)

½ cup finely chopped jicama or cucumber

2 tablespoons minced green onions (scallions)

1 teaspoon celery seed

Splash hot-pepper sauce

Salt and pepper, to taste

1. Combine all ingredients in serving bowl and mix well. Chill 3 hours or overnight.

Serving suggestion: Slice up a selection of your favorite vegetables, such as broccoli, radishes, celery, carrots, green beans, zucchini, cauliflower, endive or cucumber.

Makes 2½ cups dip

Recipe created by Chef Neil Zevnik

"Every school that has students who live in poverty must
have meals available. Children cannot learn or function properly if they are
undernourished. We should all contact our local schools and find
out what is being done to solve the problem."

CHERYL CHASE

(VOICE OF RUGRATS' ANGELICA)

PREPARATION TIME: 10 MINUTES

CHILL TIME: 2 HOURS TO OVERNIGHT

COOK TIME: 12 MINUTES

....

2 cups all-purpose flour

Pinch salt

¾ cup butter or margarine (I Can't Believe It's Not Butter!® Spread)

¾ cup sugar

1 egg

1 teaspoon vanilla extract

Decorative sprinkles and colored sugar

1. In small bowl, combine flour and salt; set aside.
2. In large bowl, with electric mixer at medium speed, beat butter or margarine with sugar until creamy.
3. Beat in egg and vanilla at medium speed. Gradually beat in flour mixture at low speed until dough forms.
4. Cover with plastic wrap; chill at least 2 hours, or until dough is firm.
5. Preheat oven to 325°F. On well-floured board, roll dough to ¼-inch thickness. Using your favorite cookie cutters, cut out cookies and arrange on ungreased cookie sheets. Decorate with sprinkles and colored sugar.
6. Bake 12 minutes, or until edges are lightly golden. Let cool on wire racks 2 minutes. Remove from racks and cool completely.

Makes 2 dozen cookies

Serving suggestion: Nothing goes better with cookies than milk.

"I don't like to see people, especially children, go hungry.
If there is anything I can do to help eradicate this problem, or even just help
in some small way, then I'll do it. I am honored just to have
been asked to help make a difference."

CHEF LEAH CHASE

SHRIMP CLEMENCEAU

PREPARATION TIME: 20 MINUTES
COOK TIME: 20 MINUTES

....

½ cup butter or margarine (I Can't Believe It's Not Butter!® Spread)

2 medium potatoes, peeled and diced

2 pounds small shrimp, peeled and deveined

½ cup button mushrooms, quartered

2 cloves garlic, finely chopped

1 cup frozen green peas

2 tablespoons chopped fresh parsley

⅓ cup dry white wine

¼ teaspoon seasoned salt (Lawry's®)

¼ teaspoon seasoned pepper (Lawry's®)

1. In a 5-quart saucepan, melt butter or margarine and cook potatoes 5 minutes, or until almost tender.
2. Add shrimp, mushrooms and garlic. Cook over medium heat, stirring occasionally, about 5 minutes, or until shrimp turn pink.
3. Stir in remaining ingredients and cook, stirring occasionally, 5 minutes, or until heated through.

Makes 4 servings

Serving suggestion: Toss together a spinach salad topped with Wish-Bone® Chunky Blue Cheese Dressing.

"To think that just one child would go to bed hungry somewhere
in this country is heartbreaking—to know just how many do is virtually
incomprehensible. This is not a problem that only exists in
the far reaches of the globe. It happens right here in our own backyard.
Together, as concerned citizens, we must do more to make sure
every child's needs are met."

KATIE COURIC

KATIE'S LEMON CHICKEN

PREPARATION TIME: 10 MINUTES

COOK TIME: 20 MINUTES

....

4 boneless, skinless chicken-breast halves, pounded thin (about 1¼ pounds)

⅓ cup plus 3 tablespoons all-purpose flour, divided

2 tablespoons butter or margarine (I Can't Believe It's Not Butter!® Spread)

2 tablespoons olive oil (Bertolli®)

3 cups chicken broth

Juice of 2 lemons (about ¼ cup)

Salt and white pepper, to taste

2 tablespoons chopped fresh parsley and 8 lemon slices, for garnish

1. Coat chicken breasts with ⅓ cup flour, shaking off excess.

2. In a 12-inch skillet, melt butter or margarine with oil over medium-high heat and cook chicken for 15 minutes, or until no longer pink, turning once. Remove chicken from skillet and set aside.

3. Stir remaining 3 tablespoons flour into pan juices in skillet. Bring to a boil and cook, stirring frequently, about 1 minute.

4. Stir in chicken broth and lemon juice. Reduce heat to low.

5. Return chicken to skillet; heat through. Add salt and pepper.

6. Garnish, if desired, with chopped fresh parsley and lemon slices.

Makes 4 servings

Serving suggestion: Lipton® Rice & Sauce (Chicken Flavor) is a quick and easy side dish.

"As a people, we value family, education and success.
Hunger is an enemy to all three. Scientific studies have demonstrated
that even brief periods of hunger can permanently inhibit a
child's mental, emotional and physical growth. Kids who are hungry
do poorly in school and are unlikely to grow into
productive adults. For families, experiencing hunger means living in
a world of isolation and shame. Caring citizens must put
an end to this national disgrace."

TED DANSON AND MARY STEENBURGEN

PREPARATION TIME: **10** MINUTES

COOK TIME: **45** MINUTES

....

4 egg whites, or ½ cup egg substitute

1 cup nonfat sour cream

1 can (8 ounces) whole kernel corn, drained

1 can (8 ounces) creamed corn

1 package (6 ounces) cornbread mix

¼ cup butter or margarine (I Can't Believe It's Not Butter!® Spread), melted

½ cup shredded reduced-fat cheddar or Swiss cheese

1. Preheat oven to 350°F. In large bowl, combine all ingredients except cheese.

2. Pour into a greased 13-inch-by-9-inch baking dish and bake 35 minutes.

3. Sprinkle with cheese and bake an additional 10 minutes, or until toothpick inserted in center comes out clean.

4. Cut into squares; serve warm.

Makes 10 servings

Serving suggestion: Add some Salsa Soup for a delicious light lunch. To make 10 servings, prepare 2 envelopes of Lipton® Soup Secrets® Ring-O-Noodle Soup Mix as directed, stirring in 1 cup prepared salsa. Garnish, if desired, with shredded cheddar cheese.

"When we think about millions of hungry children,
we don't think about America. We relate the problem to other nations, like
Ethiopia, India or Somalia. The sad truth is that is that one in six
American kids is at risk due to poor nutrition."

KRISTEN DAVIS

PREPARATION TIME: 20 MINUTES

CHILL TIME: 3 HOURS

COOK TIME: 8 MINUTES

....

2½ cups all-purpose flour

½ teaspoon salt

1 cup butter or margarine (I Can't Believe It's Not Butter!® Spread) at room temperature

⅔ cup sugar

1 egg yolk

1 teaspoon vanilla extract

1¼ teaspoons almond extract, divided

2 cups semisweet chocolate chips

¼ cup milk

Chocolate sprinkles, chopped nuts, flaked coconut or other decorations (optional)

1. In small bowl, combine flour and salt; set aside.

2. In large bowl, with electric mixer at medium speed, beat butter or margarine and sugar until creamy. Add egg yolk; beat well. Stir in vanilla and ¾ teaspoon almond extract.

3. Stir in flour mixture until dough forms. Shape into logs, about 1½ inches in diameter, and wrap in waxed paper. Chill 3 hours.

4. Preheat oven to 375°F. Slice logs into ⅛-inch-thick slices. Place on ungreased cookie sheets.

5. Bake 8 minutes, or until edges are lightly golden; remove from cookie sheets and let cool on wire racks for 2 minutes.

6. Meanwhile, make glaze. In saucepan over low heat, melt chocolate chips, milk and the remaining ½ teaspoon almond extract; stir until smooth. Remove from heat.

7. To assemble: Dip cookie halfway into warm glaze. (If glaze thickens, add milk to thin). Sprinkle, if desired, with chocolate sprinkles, chopped nuts, flaked coconut or your favorite decoration.

8. Place on cookie sheets lined with waxed paper until glaze hardens. Store cookies in airtight container.

Makes 5½ dozen cookies

Serving suggestion: Serve with hot Lipton® Tea.

"We cannot stick our heads in the sand concerning the issue
of hunger in America. Even though this subject seldom reaches the front page
of our newspapers or is featured on news programs
because of its lack of sensationalism, the problem exists in massive
proportions and must be defeated."

BRUCE DAVISON

PREPARATION TIME: 10 MINUTES

COOK TIME: 10 MINUTES

....

3 medium zucchini (about 2 pounds)

12 slices (12 ounces) Monterey Jack cheese

2 eggs, separated

1 teaspoon all-purpose flour

Pinch salt

2 tablespoons olive oil (Bertolli®)

1. Cut each zucchini in half crosswise, then slice each half lengthwise into 4 slices about ½-inch thick.

2. In microwave-safe dish, microwave zucchini and ¼ cup water on HIGH 5 minutes, stirring once; cool.

3. Place a zucchini slice on a plate. Top with a cheese slice, then another zucchini slice to make a sandwich; repeat with remaining zucchini and cheese.

5. In small bowl, whisk egg whites until frothy. Add egg yolks; beat well. Stir in flour and salt.

6. Dip each zucchini sandwich into egg mixture.

7. In a 12-inch skillet, heat oil over medium heat and cook zucchini sandwiches 3 minutes, or until golden, turning once.

8. Remove from skillet; drain on paper towels and serve.

Makes 6 servings

Serving suggestion: Dish up some steaming Lipton® Soup Secrets® Noodle Soup.

"It is inconceivable that in the richest nation in the world,
we have 30 million people at risk of hunger. I believe that if we truly make
a commitment as a nation, we can defeat hunger."

BO DEREK

PREPARATION TIME: 20 MINUTES

....

7 large tomatoes, seeded and chopped, divided

2 medium mild onions, chopped, divided

2 medium red bell peppers, chopped, divided

2 small cucumbers, peeled, seeded and diced, divided

2 cloves garlic, peeled

2 slices of bread, torn into pieces

2 tablespoons red-wine vinegar

2 tablespoons olive oil (Bertolli®)

2 tablespoons hot-pepper sauce

Salt, to taste

2 hard-boiled eggs, chopped, for garnish

1 cup croutons, for garnish

1. Reserve ½ cup each of tomatoes, onions, bell peppers and cucumbers for garnish, and set aside. In blender, combine all remaining ingredients except eggs and croutons; process at high speed until smooth. Strain, if desired, and chill until ready to serve.

2. Spoon into bowls and garnish with reserved tomatoes, onions, bell peppers, cucumbers, and hard-boiled egg or croutons, if desired. Serve cold.

Makes 8 servings

Recipe created by Ana Obregon's mother

Serving suggestion: Serve with Spanish Chicken & Rice Burritos. Prepare 1 package Lipton® Sizzle & Stir® (Spanish Chicken & Rice variety), according to package directions, with 1 pound boneless, skinless chicken breasts, cut into cubes, 1 can (14½ ounces) tomatoes in juice, undrained and chopped, and/or 1 can (15 ounces) whole kernel corn, undrained. Warm 12 (8-inch) flour tortillas. Spoon about ½ cup chicken mixture into each tortilla. Roll up and serve, if desired, with shredded lettuce, shredded cheese, sour cream, green chilies and pitted ripe olives.

"Many times, a child's struggle against hunger begins before he or she
is born because the mother is undernourished. Making sure prenatal care and
proper nutrition are available for expectant mothers in need is a
critical part of ending childhood hunger."

HECTOR ELIZONDO

HECTOR'S BAKED TOMATO PASTA

PREPARATION TIME: 20 MINUTES
COOK TIME: 20 MINUTES

....

2 pounds tomatoes, cut into thick slices

1 can (2 ounces) anchovies, undrained

Black pepper, to taste

1 pinch red-pepper flakes

½ cup extra-virgin olive oil (Bertolli®)

1 pound spaghetti or linguine

Salt, to taste

2 tablespoons chopped parsley, for garnish

¼ cup grated Parmesan cheese, for garnish

1. Preheat oven to 400°F. Arrange half of the sliced tomatoes in bottom of an ungreased 13-inch-by-9-inch baking dish and top with anchovies. Sprinkle with black pepper and red-pepper flakes. Top with remaining tomatoes and olive oil. Bake 20 minutes.

2. Meanwhile, cook and drain pasta. Place baked tomato mixture in a large serving bowl. Add salt and pepper, to taste. Toss with hot cooked pasta. Sprinkle with parsley and grated Parmesan cheese, if desired.

Makes 2 to 3 servings

Serving suggestion: Accompany with a tossed salad topped with your favorite Wish-Bone® Dressing.

"Our country offers such great opportunities for all. Unfortunately, too many hardworking citizens go day to day without enough food to eat. We can do better."

DENNIS FRANZ

PREPARATION TIME: 10 MINUTES

COOK TIME: 35 MINUTES

....

2 cans (6½ ounces each) tuna, drained

1 bag (20 ounces) frozen green peas

2 cans (10¾ ounces each) condensed cream of mushroom soup

2 cups (about ½ pound) chopped fresh mushrooms

2 cans (2.8 ounces each) french-fried onions

1. Preheat oven to 350°F. In large bowl, combine tuna, peas, soup, mushrooms and 1 can french-fried onions; mix well.

2. Pour into a 13-inch-by-9-inch ungreased baking dish, then sprinkle with remaining french-fried onions.

3. Bake 35 minutes, or until heated through.

Makes 4 servings

Serving suggestion: Enjoy with fresh-brewed iced Lipton® Tea.

"The full extent of the problem of hunger is not obvious to most of us. We see the homeless, but there are a growing number of working poor, struggling to survive, who don't have enough money to put adequate food on the table. We must find a solution to this ever-increasing problem—and quickly."

SCOTT AND CAROL GLENN

RENEE'S CHICKEN PAPRIKA

PREPARATION TIME: 15 MINUTES
COOK TIME: 1 HOUR, 15 MINUTES

⅔ cup all-purpose flour
2½ teaspoons Hungarian paprika, divided
1 teaspoon salt
¼ teaspoon black pepper
2½- to 3-pound chicken, cut into serving pieces
¼ cup olive oil (Bertolli®)
20 small button mushrooms (4 to 5 ounces)
20 pearl onions, peeled (4 ounces)
20 small red potatoes, quartered (1 pound)
20 baby carrots (6 ounces)
3 garlic cloves, finely chopped
4 cups chicken broth or water
Cayenne pepper, to taste
¼ cup finely chopped fresh parsley

1. Mix flour with 1½ teaspoons paprika, salt and pepper. Dredge chicken pieces in flour mixture.
2. In a 6-quart heavy-duty saucepot or Dutch oven, heat oil over medium-high heat and cook chicken 10 minutes, or until brown. Add vegetables and garlic, then sprinkle with the remaining 1 teaspoon paprika, and cook 5 minutes more.
3. Add broth. Bring to a boil over medium heat. Reduce heat to low and simmer, covered, stirring occasionally, 1 hour, or until chicken is tender. Season, if desired, with cayenne pepper.
4. To serve, arrange on serving platter and sprinkle with parsley.

Makes 4 servings

Recipe created by Carol Glenn's mother, Renee

Serving suggestion: Toss a Boston lettuce salad with Wish-Bone® Dressing.

"Our society is only as healthy as our most vulnerable
citizens. It is unconscionable that the weakest links in our country are our
hungry children. No other Western industrialized nation
has widespread hunger within its borders. We really must put an end
to hunger in the United States if we are to keep our
prosperity and protect the future."

LINDA GRAY

OVEN·STEAMED ASIAN·STYLE FISH

PREPARATION TIME: 10 MINUTES
CHILL TIME: 30 MINUTES
COOK TIME: 20 MINUTES

....

4 thick halibut, salmon, swordfish, red snapper, cod or sea bass fillets (about 6 ounces each)

2 cups sliced white mushrooms

2 tablespoons low-sodium soy sauce

2 tablespoons dry sherry

1 tablespoon sesame oil

1 tablespoon fresh lime juice

⅓ cup chopped green onions (scallions)

2 tablespoons chopped fresh cilantro (coriander)

1 tablespoon chopped fresh mint

2 garlic cloves, finely chopped

2 teaspoons grated fresh ginger

Cayenne pepper, to taste

1 lime, cut into wedges, for garnish

2 tablespoons whole cilantro leaves, for garnish

1. Rinse fish in cold water; pat dry. In a 13-inch-by-9-inch greased baking dish, arrange fish in a single layer and top with mushrooms.

2. In small bowl, combine all remaining ingredients except lime wedges and whole cilantro leaves; pour over fish. Cover and marinate in refrigerator 30 minutes.

3. Preheat oven to 375°F. Bake fish with marinade 20 minutes, or until it turns opaque and flakes with fork.

4. Garnish, if desired, with lime wedges and fresh cilantro leaves.

Makes 4 servings

Serving suggestion: Place fish on a bed of Lipton® Rice & Sauce (Teriyaki variety).

"The basic food needs of one in five children in the U.S.
are not being met. This poses serious long-term consequences as these
children's development is threatened. Hunger is the source
of learning disabilities and behavioral problems, which make it impossible
for hungry children to reach their potential."

STEVE GUTTENBERG

NO-FRY CHICKEN PARMESAN

PREPARATION TIME: 10 MINUTES

COOK TIME: 30 MINUTES

....

4 boneless, skinless chicken-breast halves (about 1¼ pounds)

1 egg, beaten

¾ cup Italian-seasoned dry bread crumbs

3¼ cups (26-ounce jar) marinara sauce (Ragú® Old World Style®)

1 cup shredded mozzarella cheese (about 4 ounces)

1. Preheat oven to 400°F. Dip chicken breasts in egg, then bread crumbs, coating well.

2. In a 13-inch-by-9-inch glass baking dish, arrange chicken in a single layer. Bake, uncovered, 20 minutes.

3. Pour sauce over chicken, then top with cheese. Bake an additional 10 minutes, or until chicken is no longer pink.

Makes 4 servings

Serving suggestion: Serve on top of steaming spaghetti or linguine.

"I think a grass-roots approach would be best in helping
everyday folks to work with people where they live and touch them and their
lives. A way to allow this to happen more is by working through
Hunger Free America and other organizations on a local, state and national
level. Communities don't make people, people make
communities. We could set up food banks through these organizations
and volunteers could follow up with real folks.
See the difference one person makes in a life. Hope needs
a foundation, and that foundation is you and me."

EDIE HAND

PEPPY PEANUT BUTTER BREAD

PREPARATION TIME: 15 MINUTES

COOK TIME: 50 MINUTES

....

1¾ cups all-purpose flour

2 teaspoons baking powder

½ teaspoon salt

¼ teaspoon baking soda

¾ cup creamy peanut butter (Skippy®)

⅓ cup shortening

⅔ cup sugar

2 eggs, slightly beaten

1 cup mashed ripe bananas

1. Preheat oven to 350°F. Sift flour, baking powder, salt and baking soda into medium bowl; set aside.
2. In large bowl, with electric mixer at medium speed, beat peanut butter and shortening until smooth.
3. Beat in sugar until creamy. Beat in eggs, one at a time, until blended.
4. Stir dry ingredients into batter, alternating with mashed bananas just until combined. Do not overmix.
5. Spoon into greased 9-inch-by-5-inch-by-3-inch loaf pan.
6. Bake 50 minutes, or until toothpick inserted in center comes out clean. Cool completely on wire rack.

Makes 1 loaf

Serving suggestion: Serve with cups of steaming Lipton® Tea to create a great snack.

"In the long run, taking care of the needs of America's children will cost a lot less than trying to deal with them as adults with learning disabilities and behavioral problems as a result of poor nutrition in their early years. Eliminating this problem is an investment in the future of our country."

MARIEL HEMINGWAY

SESAME BROCCOLI STIR-FRY

PREPARATION TIME: 15 MINUTES
COOK TIME: 20 MINUTES

....

Juice of 2 limes (about ¼ cup)

2 tablespoons coarsely chopped fresh ginger, plus 1 teaspoon finely chopped

2 cups (about 1 pound) broccoli florets

1 teaspoon cornstarch

½ teaspoon sesame oil

4 garlic cloves, chopped

2 green onions (scallions), sliced

1 cup (about 3 ounces) thinly sliced shiitake mushrooms

1 medium red bell pepper, cut into thin 2-inch-long strips

½ carrot, cut into ½-inch-thick slices

¼ cup low-sodium soy sauce

3 tablespoons mirin or water

2 tablespoons rice vinegar

4 cups (about ¾ pound) shredded romaine lettuce

1 teaspoon black or regular sesame seeds

1. Fill a 3-quart saucepan with water. Add lime juice and coarsely chopped ginger and bring to a boil.

2. Add broccoli and cook 1 minute, or until bright green. Drain and rinse with cold water; set aside.

3. In small bowl, stir together ¼ cup water and cornstarch until dissolved.

4. In a 12-inch skillet, heat sesame oil over medium heat and cook garlic, finely chopped ginger, green onions, mushrooms, red pepper and carrot, stirring occasionally, 2 minutes, or until crisp-tender.

5. Stir in soy sauce, mirin and vinegar and cook 2 minutes. Stir in cornstarch mixture. Bring to a boil and simmer, stirring frequently, 30 seconds, or until thickened.

6. Stir in broccoli; heat through.

7. To serve, arrange vegetables over lettuce and sprinkle with sesame seeds.

Makes 4 servings

Serving suggestion: Frosty glasses of iced Lipton® Green Tea will complement the flavors of this dish.

"No one in this country need go hungry, and alleviating
the problem is primarily a matter of readjusting our priorities. In both
the government and the private sector, self-interest has
displaced the ideal of community that made this country great. The old world
view of 'us, we, our' has been replaced by 'I, me, mine.'
The reasons for this are manifold and complex, but at the end of the day,
we need to remember that if one of us is suffering needlessly,
all of us are diminished."

DON HENLEY

HIGH SUMMER RISOTTO

PREPARATION TIME: 10 MINUTES

COOK TIME: 40 MINUTES

STAND TIME: 10 MINUTES

....

2 tablespoons olive oil (Bertolli®)

1 medium onion, chopped

¼ cup each finely chopped fresh basil and fresh parsley

2 tablespoons finely chopped fresh sage

2 cups Arborio rice

½ cup dry white wine

2½ cups (about 3 to 4 large) peeled, seeded and chopped tomatoes, divided

4 cups chicken broth

½ cup grated Parmesan cheese

2 cloves garlic, minced

2 tablespoons julienned basil leaves

Salt and freshly ground white pepper, to taste

1. In a 5- to 6-quart saucepot over medium-low heat, heat oil. Add onion, chopped basil, parsley and sage; cook until onion is tender.

2. Add rice and cook, stirring frequently, until rice is translucent. Stir in wine.

3. After most of wine is absorbed, stir in 1¼ cups tomatoes. Cook, stirring frequently, until liquid is absorbed. Meanwhile, in a separate pot, heat chicken broth.

4. Add hot chicken broth to rice mixture, ½ cup at a time. Let rice absorb broth before adding more, cooking just until mixture is thickened and creamy. You may not need all the broth.

5. When rice is tender and sauce is thick, remove from heat and stir in cheese, the remaining tomatoes, garlic and julienned basil leaves. Add salt and pepper, to taste. Cover and let stand 10 minutes; serve.

Makes 4 to 6 servings

Serving suggestion: Serve with Lipton® Iced Tea.

"In this country of the bountiful harvest, everyone can have enough to eat—we have it! We grow enough for everyone. Let's share it by supporting our local food banks, houses of worship and organizations that help!"

CATHERINE HICKS

PREPARATION TIME: 5 MINUTES
COOK TIME: 5 MINUTES
CHILL TIME: 30 MINUTES

....

1 envelope unflavored gelatin
1 cup fresh-squeezed orange juice
2 cups (1 pint) whipping or heavy cream
Fresh strawberries
Citrus peel strips, for garnish

1. In small saucepan, sprinkle unflavored gelatin over ¼ cup cold water; let stand 1 minute.
2. Stir over low heat until gelatin is completely dissolved, about 5 minutes. Stir in orange juice; let cool.
3. Pour gelatin mixture into bowl; chill until almost set, about 30 minutes.
4. Meanwhile, in large bowl, whip cream. Fold into chilled gelatin mixture.
5. To serve, spoon charlotte over strawberries and garnish with citrus peel.

Makes 4 servings

Serving suggestion: Cups of piping hot, fresh-brewed Lipton® Tea make a good accompaniment.

"It's appalling that there should be hunger anywhere
in the world, but particularly in a country like America, where there is
also such great wealth."

ELIZABETH HURLEY

SHEPHERD'S PIE

PREPARATION TIME: 10 MINUTES

COOK TIME: 1 HOUR, 15 MINUTES

....

2 tablespoons olive oil (Bertolli®)

1 large onion, chopped

2 pounds ground lamb

4 large carrots, diced

1 cup dry red wine

4 sprigs fresh rosemary

1 tablespoon tomato paste

2 cups chicken broth

Salt and pepper, to taste

4 pounds potatoes

8 tablespoons butter or margarine (I Can't Believe It's Not Butter!® Spread)

⅓ to ½ cup milk

1. In a 12-inch skillet over medium-high heat, heat oil and cook onion until tender. Stir in lamb and cook until lamb is no longer pink; drain excess oil.

2. Stir in carrots, wine and rosemary. Bring to a boil and cook, 5 minutes, stirring occasionally.

3. Stir in tomato paste, chicken broth and salt and pepper. Bring to a boil over high heat. Reduce heat and simmer, covered, 30 minutes, stirring occasionally. Add a few tablespoons of broth to prevent sticking, if necessary.

4. Meanwhile, in large stockpot, boil potatoes until tender; drain. Mash potatoes with butter or margarine, milk and salt and pepper, to taste.

5. Preheat oven to 375°F. Spoon lamb mixture into ungreased 3-quart casserole dish. Top with mashed potatoes, then spread smooth. Score topping with fork.

6. Bake 30 minutes, or until casserole is bubbling and potatoes are golden.

Makes 6 servings

Serving suggestion: Salad topped with Wish-Bone® Dressing makes a tasty side dish.

"Twelve million children in the United States face hunger every day. Bringing an end to this terrible situation is a passion I share with my friends at the Entertainment Industry Foundation. Together we can end hunger."

KATHY IRELAND

PREPARATION TIME: 15 MINUTES

COOK TIME: 15 MINUTES

....

2½ cups uncooked quick or old-fashioned oats

2 cups all-purpose flour

½ teaspoon salt

1 teaspoon baking powder

1 teaspoon baking soda

1 cup butter or margarine (I Can't Believe It's Not Butter!® Spread)

1 cup granulated sugar

1 cup firmly packed brown sugar

2 eggs

1 teaspoon vanilla extract

1 bag (12 ounces) semisweet chocolate chips

3 cups unsalted macadamia nuts

1. Preheat oven to 350°F. In blender or food processor, process oats in small batches to form coarse crumbs.

2. In medium bowl, combine oats, flour, salt, baking powder and baking soda; set aside.

3. In large bowl, with electric mixer at medium speed, beat butter or margarine and sugars together until creamy. Beat in eggs and vanilla, scraping sides occasionally. Gradually beat in oat mixture until blended.

4. Stir in chocolate chips and nuts. Drop dough by tablespoonfuls onto ungreased cookie sheets.

5. Bake 12 to 15 minutes, or until golden brown. Let stand on cookie sheets 2 minutes. Then transfer to a wire rack to cool completely.

Makes about 3½ dozen

"Most Americans think of hunger as a problem
affecting only places like India, Africa or South America. But it is
a tragic reality that our country has millions of children
who are suffering from lack of food. We must all work together to
save our country from this problem!"

BEVERLY JOHNSON

PREPARATION TIME: 20 MINUTES

COOK TIME: 20 MINUTES

....

2 tablespoons olive oil (Bertolli®)

3 cloves garlic, finely chopped

3¼ cups (26-ounce jar) pasta sauce (Ragú® Robusto!™)

1 teaspoon dried basil leaves, crushed

½ cup dry white wine

1 package (16 ounces) linguine

4 cans (6½ ounces each) chopped clams, drained, with 1½ cups liquid reserved

1 tablespoon freshly grated lemon peel

1. In medium saucepan, heat oil over low heat and cook garlic for 1 minute. Add pasta sauce, basil, white wine and reserved clam liquid.

2. Simmer, uncovered, over medium heat 15 minutes, stirring occasionally. Meanwhile, cook pasta. Drain and keep warm.

3. Stir clams into sauce and cook 2 minutes, or until clams are heated through.

4. To serve, spoon clam sauce over hot pasta and garnish, if desired, with lemon peel.

Makes 6 servings

"Hunger is a silent crisis affecting families across America.
Millions of families do not have incomes high enough to meet their basic needs.
In a wealthy nation like ours, there is no justification for this neglect.
Children are especially vulnerable. They deserve adequate nutrition in
order to grow and prosper. Yet the USDA estimates
that 12 million children suffer from hunger and the developmental
problems caused by the lack of proper nutrition.
Hungry children are unable to pay attention in school, unable to fight
common childhood illnesses and unable to reach their
full potential. It is irresponsible and unconscionable to force children
to go without the food, housing and medical care that they need
and deserve. I commend the leadership of the End Hunger Network for
all that it is doing to achieve this very important goal."

SENATOR EDWARD M. KENNEDY

CAPE COD FISH CHOWDER

PREPARATION TIME: 15 MINUTES

COOK TIME: 55 MINUTES

....

2 ounces salt pork or bacon, chopped

2 medium onions, sliced

1½ pounds cod or scrod fillets, cut into chunks

4 large potatoes, diced

1 cup (about 2 stalks) chopped celery

1 bay leaf

1 teaspoon salt

2 cups milk

2 tablespoons butter or margarine (I Can't Believe It's Not Butter!® Spread)

Pepper, to taste

1. In a 4-quart saucepot, cook salt pork until golden or cook bacon until done; remove and set aside. Add onions and cook until lightly browned.

2. Add 2 cups water, fish, potatoes, celery, bay leaf and salt, and cook, covered, 40 minutes. Add milk and butter or margarine, and cook for an additional 5 minutes, until hot. Remove bay leaf. Season with pepper and serve.

Makes 10 servings

"To be concerned about hunger requires a change of personal life-style; more inclusive, less exclusive. Converting habits that harm into resources that heal; eating less, sharing more—only then do we have the right to influence public policy. 'Whosoever boasts about giving is like clouds and wind without rain (Proverbs 24:14).'"

GRAHAM KERR

SWEET POTATO PIE

CHILL TIME: OVERNIGHT

PREPARATION TIME: 20 MINUTES

COOK TIME: 53 MINUTES

STAND TIME: 15 MINUTES

....

¾ cup low-fat vanilla yogurt

½ Basic Pie Crust recipe (see below)

3 medium sweet potatoes (about 1½ pounds), cooked, peeled and mashed

1 tablespoon margarine (I Can't Believe It's Not Butter!® Spread)

½ cup egg substitute, or 2 eggs

¼ cup firmly packed brown sugar

1 tablespoon molasses

¾ cup evaporated skim milk

¼ teaspoon each ground nutmeg, cinnamon and ginger

1 teaspoon maple syrup

1. One day before serving, place yogurt in strainer lined with cheesecloth. Set strainer over a bowl, refrigerate, and allow the yogurt to drain overnight. Discard liquid.

2. The day of serving, preheat oven to 425°F. Roll pastry into a 10-inch circle. Press into a 9-inch pie pan and crimp edges. Pierce with fork. Place a piece of waxed paper on the pastry and pour in enough dried beans to cover the bottom. Bake 8 minutes, or until golden. Remove from oven; gently remove waxed paper and beans. Let stand on wire rack.

3. Meanwhile, combine sweet potatoes, margarine, egg substitute, brown sugar, molasses, evaporated milk and spices. Pour into baked pastry and smooth. Cover the rim of the pastry with strips of aluminum foil.

4. Bake 45 minutes, or until knife inserted in center comes out clean. On wire rack, cool 15 minutes.

5. Meanwhile, blend drained yogurt with maple syrup. Serve each slice of pie with a dollop of yogurt topping.

Basic Pie Crust: In food processor, process 1½ cups cake flour, 1 teaspoon sugar and ⅛ teaspoon salt. Pour in 2 tablespoons extra-light olive oil (Bertolli®) and pulse until mixed. Add ¼ cup stick butter or margarine (I Can't Believe It's Not Butter!® Spread), cut into small pieces, and pulse until mixed. Pulse 10 times, or until crumbs are size of small peas. Pour in 1 teaspoon vinegar and 4 tablespoons ice water and pulse until dough starts to form a ball. Shape into 2 balls. Wrap in plastic wrap and chill at least 30 minutes before using. Note: Makes enough for 2 crusts; reserve half of dough for another use.

Makes 8 servings

Serving suggestion: Accompany with tall glasses of fresh-brewed iced Lipton® Tea.

"There is a hidden epidemic threatening the lives of millions of Americans...hunger. In this land of plenty, it is unthinkable that fellow citizens are going hungry. Included among these millions are children who, due to malnourishment, are not developing to their full potential intellectually, emotionally or behaviorally. The fortunate must provide for the less fortunate, and I am eager to contribute to this cause."

SWOOSIE KURTZ

EGGPLANT A LA SWOOSE

PREPARATION TIME: 10 MINUTES
COOK TIME: 45 MINUTES

....

1 large eggplant

4 tablespoons butter or margarine (I Can't Believe It's Not Butter!® Spread), divided

1 pound ground beef

¾ cup chopped onion (about 1½ onions)

½ cup chopped green bell pepper (about ½ pepper)

1 cup tomato sauce (Ragú® Old World Style®)

4 tablespoons bread crumbs, divided

1 teaspoon salt

¼ teaspoon dried oregano leaves

Black pepper, to taste

2 tablespoons grated Parmesan cheese

1. Preheat oven to 375°F. Halve eggplant lengthwise. Scoop out flesh, leaving ½-inch shells. Cut flesh into large pieces; reserve eggplant shells.

2. In a 12-inch skillet, melt 1 tablespoon butter or margarine and brown ground beef. Add onion and green pepper and cook until tender. Remove from skillet and set aside.

3. In the same skillet, melt the remaining 3 tablespoons butter or margarine and cook eggplant pieces until tender.

4. In a large bowl, combine beef mixture, eggplant, tomato sauce, 2 tablespoons of the bread crumbs, salt, oregano and pepper.

5. Spoon mixture into reserved eggplant shells; sprinkle with cheese and the remaining 2 tablespoons bread crumbs.

6. Bake 30 minutes, or until bubbly and golden brown.

Makes 6 servings

"Our great country is rich and abundant in so many ways. It is totally unacceptable to me that we have children and families going hungry! I eagerly add my voice in support of this important issue."

DIANE LADD

DIANE'S SOUTHERN JAPANESE DISH

PREPARATION TIME: 20 MINUTES
COOK TIME: 35 MINUTES

....

6 tablespoons olive oil (Bertolli®), divided
1 medium onion, chopped
½ green bell pepper, chopped
4 carrots, thinly sliced
1 cup (about 4 ounces) chopped green beans
1 medium potato, unpeeled and diced
½ rutabaga, peeled and thinly sliced
½ turnip, peeled and thinly sliced
3 cloves garlic, finely chopped
⅔ cup soy sauce or tamari sauce, divided
½ medium eggplant, cut into ½-inch cubes
1 medium zucchini, halved lengthwise and cut into ½-inch-thick pieces
2 small yellow squash, halved lengthwise and cut into ½-inch-thick pieces
¼ head green cabbage, cut into strips
¼ head cauliflower, cut into florets
1 package (15 ounces) firm tofu, cut into ½-inch cubes
1 package (10 ounces) fresh spinach leaves, trimmed, rinsed and patted dry
8 ounces mozzarella cheese, sliced ⅛-inch thick

1. In a 12-inch nonstick skillet, heat 3 tablespoons oil. Stir in onion, green pepper, carrots, green beans, potato, rutabaga, turnip, garlic, ⅓ cup soy sauce and ⅓ cup water. Cover and bring to a boil. Cook over medium heat, stirring occasionally, until vegetables are tender, about 15 minutes.

2. Stir in the remaining 3 tablespoons oil, the remaining ⅓ cup soy sauce, ⅓ cup water and all remaining vegetables except for spinach. Simmer, covered, stirring occasionally, 10 minutes, or until vegetables are tender.

3. Stir in tofu. Arrange spinach on vegetable mixture, then top with mozzarella. Simmer until spinach is wilted and cheese is melted.

Makes 8 servings

Serving suggestion: Enjoy with iced Lipton® Green Tea.

"What can I do to help? I am asking my senator to support political action to end hunger in the greatest country on this planet."

MARTIN LANDAU

PREPARATION TIME: 5 MINUTES

COOK TIME: 18 MINUTES

CHILL TIME: 6 TO 24 HOURS

....

¾ cup Italian salad dressing (Wish-Bone®)

1 tablespoon Worcestershire sauce

1 tablespoon firmly packed brown sugar

1 large jalapeño pepper, seeded and finely chopped

1 teaspoon ground allspice

1 teaspoon ground ginger

1 beef top round steak, 1 inch thick (about 1½ pounds)

1. For marinade, combine all ingredients except steak. In large, shallow nonaluminum baking dish or plastic bag, pour ½ cup marinade over steak; turn to coat. Cover, or close bag, and marinate in refrigerator, turning occasionally, 6 to 24 hours. Refrigerate remaining marinade separately.

2. Remove steak from marinade, discarding marinade in dish or bag.

3. Grill steak, turning occasionally and brushing frequently with the marinade that was reserved in the refrigerator, 16 to 18 minutes, or until steak is medium-rare to medium doneness.

Makes 4 servings

"I know this will work because
this recipe ended hunger in our family."

JAY LENO

UNCLE LOUIE'S CHICKEN WINGS MARINARA

PREPARATION TIME: 10 MINUTES
COOK TIME: 45 MINUTES

....

3 pounds chicken wings

¼ cup olive oil (Bertolli®), divided

1 clove garlic, finely chopped

1 can (14 ounces) Italian plum tomatoes, drained and crushed

1 tablespoon chopped fresh parsley

1½ teaspoons salt

2 to 4 tablespoons hot-pepper sauce

1. Preheat oven to 425°F. Cut tips off chicken wings, then cut wings in half at joint. Arrange on aluminum foil-lined cookie sheet and bake 45 minutes, or until golden brown; set aside and cover with foil to keep warm.

2. Meanwhile, in a 2-quart saucepan, heat oil and cook garlic, tomatoes, parsley and salt, stirring occasionally, 20 minutes.

3. Add hot-pepper sauce and cook 3 minutes more.

4. In large bowl, toss chicken wings with ½ cup sauce.

5. Serve with remaining sauce for dipping.

Makes about 36 wings

Serving suggestion: For variety, use Wish-Bone® Chunky Blue Cheese Dressing as an additional dipping sauce and serve with celery stalks.

"There are easy, everyday choices we can make to help end
hunger in America:
1) Support local, organic and sustainable agriculture.
2) Use unrefined and minimally processed ingredients.
3) Make one meal (or more) each day a vegetarian meal.
These simple choices have multiple rewards!
They help conserve our precious resources and provide you and your
family with high-quality nutritious foods. Go to your local farmer's markets.
Ask your local markets to carry more organic foods.
Educate yourself and your community. Be a voice and a light!"

KENNY LOGGINS

PREPARATION TIME: 20 MINUTES

....

¾ cup chopped flat-leaf parsley

¾ cup chopped fresh cilantro (coriander)

¼ cup fresh lemon juice

¼ cup olive oil (Bertolli®)

1 tablespoon fresh chopped ginger

2 teaspoons peanut oil

1 clove garlic, finely chopped

Sea salt or tamari, to taste

8 ounces pasta, cooked, drained and kept hot

1. In blender or food processor, blend all ingredients except pasta until smooth, adding additional oil if sauce is too thick.

2. Toss with hot pasta and serve.

Makes 4 servings

Recipe created by chef Susan Van Amburgh

Serving suggestion: A tossed green salad with Wish-Bone® Dressing makes a delicious side dish.

"To know that children are suffering and going without food
is intolerable in a society such as ours. I hope that all of our leaders,
in both the public and private sectors, will work tirelessly
to eradicate hunger. We all have a responsibility to bring back life to our most
precious natural resource."

JOAN LUNDEN

BUTTERNUT SQUASH SOUP

PREPARATION TIME: 10 MINUTES
COOK TIME: 1 HOUR

....

1 medium butternut squash (about 2¼ pounds)

1 tablespoon butter or margarine (I Can't Believe It's Not Butter!® Spread)

1 medium onion, chopped

1 teaspoon to 1 tablespoon grated fresh ginger

3 cups chicken broth

Salt and pepper, to taste

6 tablespoons low-fat sour cream, for garnish

6 apple slices, for garnish

1. Preheat oven to 400°F. Halve squash lengthwise; discard seeds.

2. Arrange squash halves, cut-side-down, on baking pan coated with nonstick cooking spray.

3. Bake 40 minutes, or until very tender; remove from oven and let cool. Remove pulp from skin; set aside.

4. Meanwhile, in saucepan over medium heat, melt butter or margarine. Add onion and ginger; cook 5 minutes, or until onion is tender.

5. Add broth and simmer, covered, 10 minutes. Add squash pulp; mix well.

6. In blender or food processor, process squash mixture until smooth. Return soup to saucepan and add 1 to 2 cups water to reach desired consistency; heat through over low heat.

7. Garnish, if desired, with low-fat sour cream and apple slices.

Makes 6 servings

Serving suggestion: For lunch or a light dinner, serve with Classic Waldorf Salad. To make 6 servings, in medium bowl, blend ½ cup Hellmann's® or Best Foods® Mayonnaise, 1 tablespoon sugar, 1 tablespoon fresh lemon juice and ⅛ teaspoon salt. Stir in 3 medium apples (cored and diced) and 1 cup (about 2 stalks) chopped celery. Cover and chill at least 30 minutes to blend flavors. Just before serving, sprinkle with ½ cup chopped walnuts.

"Every child should be given the right to grow up and become
a productive citizen. This will not happen unless, at the very least, basic food
needs are met. Ending childhood hunger should be a national priority."

PAMELA SUE MARTIN

SUMMER SUNDAE ICE CREAM PIE

PREPARATION TIME: 10 MINUTES

CHILL TIME: 30 MINUTES

....

½ gallon vanilla ice cream (Breyers®), slightly softened

9-inch chocolate-crumb crust or graham-cracker crust

½ cup peanut butter (Skippy®), melted

2 tablespoons chocolate sprinkles

Additional sundae toppings (optional)

1. Scoop ice cream into prepared crust.

2. Drizzle with melted peanut butter and top with sprinkles.

3. Cover and freeze until ready to serve. Let stand 5 minutes before slicing. Garnish, if desired, with your favorite sundae toppings and serve.

Makes 8 to 10 servings

"It saddens me to think that there are children in America
who are hungry every day of their lives. No one can live—and grow—without
such a fundamental necessity as food. If we Americans reach out
to our own communities, we could end this crisis."

TIM McGRAW

CHICKEN AND DUMPLINGS

PREPARATION TIME: 20 MINUTES

COOK TIME: 2 HOURS, 20 MINUTES TO 3 HOURS, 20 MINUTES

....

1 soup chicken (4 to 5 pounds), cut into pieces

1 teaspoon salt

1 teaspoon thyme leaves

½ teaspoon pepper

4 carrots, sliced

1 cup flour

Pinch salt

¼ cup milk

1 egg

1. In a 5- to 6-quart stockpot, combine chicken, 8 cups water, salt, thyme and pepper; bring to a boil over high heat. Reduce heat and simmer, covered, 2 to 3 hours, or until tender, stirring occasionally.

2. Remove chicken from pot. Strip meat from bones and return to broth; stir in carrots and simmer 15 minutes, or until carrots are tender.

3. Meanwhile, in small bowl, combine flour, salt, milk and egg. Mix to form dough. Roll dough ⅛-inch thick on floured board. Cut into 1- to 2-inch squares and drop, one by one, into broth.

4. Simmered, covered, 5 minutes, or until dumplings are done. Season, if desired, with additional salt and pepper.

Makes 6 servings

Serving suggestion: Serve with warm rolls topped with I Can't Believe It's Not Butter!® Spread.

"We cannot stand by and allow the future of our country to be undermined by the reality of American children going hungry! Please join in to help the 12 million children who are malnourished in our country!"

DONNA MILLS

CREAM CHEESE PIE WITH APRICOT GLAZE

PREPARATION TIME: 20 MINUTES

COOK TIME: 55 MINUTES

CHILL TIME: 5 HOURS TO OVERNIGHT

....

6 tablespoons butter or margarine (I Can't Believe It's Not Butter!® Spread), melted

1¼ cups plus 3 tablespoons sugar, divided

1½ cups graham-cracker crumbs

2 packages (8 ounces each) cream cheese, softened

2 eggs

3 teaspoons vanilla extract, divided

2 teaspoons fresh lemon juice, divided

1 teaspoon grated lemon peel

1 cup sour cream, at room temperature

1 can (16 ounces) apricot halves in syrup

1 tablespoon cornstarch

Yellow and red food coloring (optional)

1. Preheat oven to 300°F. To make crust, combine butter or margarine, ¼ cup sugar and crumbs in bowl. Press onto bottom and sides of ungreased 9-inch pie plate. Bake 10 minutes; set aside.

2. Meanwhile, in large bowl, with electric mixer at medium speed, beat cream cheese until smooth. Beat in ¾ cup sugar, eggs, 2 teaspoons vanilla extract, 1 teaspoon lemon juice and peel until blended. Pour into crust.

3. Bake 40 minutes, or until center is set. (Filling may crack but should not brown.)

4. Meanwhile, in small bowl, blend sour cream, ¼ cup sugar and 1 teaspoon vanilla extract. Carefully spread over top of pie, then bake 5 minutes.

5. Cool pie on wire rack at least 30 minutes. Chill 5 hours or overnight.

6. To make glaze, drain apricots, reserving ¾ cup syrup.

7. In small saucepan, combine the remaining 3 tablespoons sugar and cornstarch; stir in reserved syrup.

8. Cook over medium heat, stirring frequently, until mixture is thickened and clear.

9. Remove from heat; stir in the remaining ingredients. Spoon into small bowl and cover with waxed paper touching surface of glaze; chill until cool.

10. Arrange apricot halves, cut-side-down, in ring on top of pie, then spoon on glaze.

Makes 8 servings

Serving suggestion: Serve with cups of hot Lipton® Tea for an elegant end to any meal.

"It is unconscionable for children in our prosperous country,
or anywhere for that matter, to go without food. I implore every reader of this
book to contact their local and state representatives to
encourage action to end hunger."

KEVIN NEALON

PREPARATION TIME: 10 MINUTES

COOK TIME: 1 HOUR, 10 MINUTES

....

1 tablespoon olive oil (Bertolli®)

1 large onion, diced

4 medium green bell peppers, chopped

3 cans (28 ounces each) crushed tomatoes

2 cans (19 ounces each) dark red kidney beans, drained

3 tablespoons chili powder

1 tablespoon sugar

1 teaspoon salt

1. In a 6-quart stockpot, heat oil over medium heat and cook onion and peppers, stirring occasionally, 5 minutes, or until crisp-tender.

2. Stir in remaining ingredients. Bring to a boil over high heat. Reduce heat and simmer, covered, stirring occasionally, 1 hour.

Makes 8 servings

Serving suggestion: Round out the meal with toasty Mexican Pizza Bagels. To make 8 servings, preheat oven to 350°F. On ungreased baking sheet, arrange 8 bagels that have already been halved and toasted. Evenly spread about ¼ cup Ragú® Old World Style® Pasta Sauce on each half, then top each with about ⅛ cup shredded Monterey Jack cheese with jalapeño peppers. Bake 10 minutes, or until cheese is melted.

"If in some small way, I can help eradicate hunger in our nation
by being part of such a worthy endeavor, it is indeed my pleasure. It is an
embarrassment that the United States, the wealthiest nation,
has people that go hungry."

CRAIG T. NELSON

PREPARATION TIME: 15 MINUTES
COOK TIME: 21 MINUTES

....

½ cup barbecue sauce

½ cup Worcestershire sauce

1¼ cups extra-light olive oil (Bertolli®), divided

10 bone-in skinless chicken thighs (about 2 pounds)

6 flour tortillas

3 medium avocados, peeled and mashed

1 jar (12 ounces) medium salsa, divided

1 Maui or Spanish onion, finely chopped

4 green onions (scallions), finely chopped

1. In small bowl, blend barbecue sauce and Worcestershire sauce; set aside.

2. In a 12-inch skillet, heat 1 cup oil and fry chicken, in 2 batches, turning once and basting with barbecue sauce mixture, 20 minutes, or until chicken is no longer pink. Drain on paper towels; let cool.

3. Meanwhile, in another 12-inch skillet, heat remaining ¼ cup oil and fry tortillas, turning once, until golden, about 1 minute. Drain on paper towels. Arrange on cookie sheet and cover to keep warm.

4. Remove chicken from bone and coarsely chop; set aside.

5. In medium bowl, combine avocados, ¼ cup salsa and onion.

6. To serve, arrange chicken on tortillas and top with avocado mixture and remaining salsa.

Makes 6 servings

Serving suggestion: Lipton® Rice & Sauce (Spanish variety) makes a tasty side dish.

"The world produces enough food to feed the entire population. It's a travesty that anyone should go hungry anywhere."

DONNY OSMOND

PREPARATION TIME: 20 MINUTES

COOK TIME: 40 MINUTES

....

2 tablespoons olive oil (Bertolli®)

12 corn tortillas

1 pound boneless, skinless, chicken-breast halves, cooked and chopped

2 cans (10¾ ounces each) condensed cream of chicken soup

1 container (8 ounces) sour cream

4 cups (about 16 ounces) cheddar or Monterey Jack cheese, shredded

½ cup chopped green onions (scallions)

1. Preheat oven to 350°F. In a 12-inch skillet, heat oil and cook tortillas, one or two at a time, until heated through, turning once. Arrange on paper towels.

2. In medium bowl, combine chicken, soup and sour cream and mix well.

3. In a 2-quart baking dish, layer tortillas, 3½ cups cheese and chicken mixture, ending with a layer of tortillas. Sprinkle with the remaining ½ cup cheese.

4. Bake 30 minutes, or until heated through. Sprinkle with green onions.

Makes 6 servings

Recipe created by Debbie Osmond, Donny's wife

Serving suggestion: Serve with tomatoes topped with Wish-Bone® Italian Dressing.

"I went to bed hungry many nights as a child.
It was a Dream that dressed me up when I was ragged, and it was a Dream
that filled me up when I was hungry. Now it's my
Dream to see that no child in this world ever goes hungry, certainly
not here in America, the most bountiful country in the world.
We can do better...we must! What can I do?"

DOLLY PARTON

PREPARATION TIME: 10 MINUTES

COOK TIME: 35 MINUTES

CHILL TIME: 1 HOUR

3 eggs, separated

1 cup sugar, divided

1 tablespoon all-purpose flour

4 cups milk

1 teaspoon vanilla extract

¼ teaspoon ground nutmeg (optional)

1. In medium bowl, with electric mixer at medium speed, beat egg yolks with ⅔ cup sugar until light and smooth. Beat in flour; set aside.

2. In small saucepan, heat milk just until boiling. With wire whisk or fork, slowly stir in egg mixture and cook, stirring constantly, 20 minutes, or until thickened. Remove from heat and stir in vanilla. Pour custard into serving bowl. Cover with plastic wrap pressed onto surface to prevent skin from forming, then refrigerate at least 1 hour, or until ready to serve.

3. Before serving, in medium bowl, with electric mixer at high speed, beat egg whites with the remaining ⅓ cup sugar until stiff.

4. Fill a nonstick skillet three-quarters full with water. Bring to a boil.

5. To make meringues, drop egg whites by tablespoonfuls into boiling water. Cook 3 minutes, or until cooked and hardened, turning once. With slotted spoon, remove meringues and arrange on custard mixture.

6. Sprinkle with nutmeg. Chill until ready to serve.

Makes 8 servings

Serving suggestion: Enjoy with cups of freshly brewed hot Lipton® Tea.

"We say the United States is a rich country, but how can we be rich when millions of poor American children go to bed hungry?"

ALEXANDRA PAUL

PREPARATION TIME: 15 MINUTES

COOK TIME: 40 MINUTES

....

1 cup all-purpose flour

1 tablespoon baking powder

½ cup unsweetened cocoa, divided

¼ teaspoon salt

1¼ cups sugar, divided

½ cup margarine (I Can't Believe It's Not Butter!® Spread), melted

½ cup soy milk or regular milk

1 teaspoon vanilla extract

1. Preheat oven to 350°F. To make cake batter, in large bowl, combine flour, baking powder, ¼ cup cocoa and salt.

2. Stir in ½ cup sugar, margarine, milk and vanilla until blended. Spoon into greased 1½-quart casserole; set aside.

3. To make sauce, bring 1½ cups water to a boil. Meanwhile, in medium bowl, combine the remaining ¾ cup sugar and ¼ cup cocoa; sprinkle over batter.

4. Carefully pour boiling water over top of batter. Do not mix.

5. Bake 40 minutes, or until toothpick inserted 1 inch into cake comes out clean.

6. Cool on wire rack 5 minutes.

7. To serve, spoon into dessert dishes.

Makes 6 servings

Reprinted with permission from *How It All Vegan!: Irresistible Recipes for an Animal-Free Diet (www.govegan.net)* by Tanya Bernard and Sarah Kramer (Arsenal Pulp Press, 1999)

Chef's serving suggestion: Top with a scoop of Breyers® Natural Vanilla Ice Cream and fresh raspberries.

"Ending hunger also means providing knowledge about
proper nutrition. That's why it's important to teach people how to shop,
prepare and preserve food."

CHEF PEPIN

PICADILLO PERFECTO

PREPARATION TIME: 10 MINUTES

COOK TIME: 30 MINUTES

....

1 pound lean ground beef

3 cloves garlic, minced

⅛ teaspoon pepper

1 cube beef bouillon (Knorr®), dissolved in ½ cup hot water

1 packet sazon with coriander and annatto (Knorr®)

1 large red bell pepper, diced

1 large onion, finely chopped

1 cup tomato sauce (Ragú® Old World Style® Traditional)

½ cup green manzanilla olives stuffed with pimiento

¼ cup dark raisins

1. In a 12-inch skillet, brown beef; drain.

2. Add garlic, pepper, bouillon and sazon; mix well.
Add bell pepper and onion.

3. Cook 5 minutes, or until onion is translucent.
Add sauce, olives and raisins.

4. Reduce heat to low and simmer, covered, 20 minutes,
stirring occasionally.

Makes 2 servings

"How unthinkable that in a country of such bursting plenty,
so many people are facing ongoing hunger and poverty. If we are truly each
other's keepers, let's support school lunches, food stamps,
neighborhood garden projects and so many other wonderful programs working
to put an end to this cruel and needless blight once and for all.
We can do it, and I'm proud to help!"

BONNIE RAITT

SWEET POTATO SALAD

PREPARATION TIME: 30 MINUTES

COOK TIME: 15 MINUTES

....

2 pounds sweet potatoes, peeled and cut into 1-inch cubes

1 teaspoon salt, plus more, to taste

1 medium red onion, sliced

½ red bell pepper, seeded and chopped

½ yellow bell pepper, seeded and chopped

¼ cup chopped fresh parsley

2½ tablespoons ketchup

3 tablespoons Dijon mustard

1 teaspoon finely chopped garlic

¾ cup olive oil (Bertolli®)

¼ cup dark cider vinegar or balsamic vinegar

1 tablespoon Worcestershire sauce

Juice of 1 lime

Black pepper, to taste

1. In large stockpot, place potatoes and enough water to cover; add 1 teaspoon salt and bring to boil. Cook 10 minutes, or until potatoes are tender. Drain and rinse with cold water until completely cool.

2. In large bowl, combine potatoes, onion, peppers and parsley; set aside.

3. In small bowl, blend ketchup, mustard and garlic. While stirring, drizzle in oil, then vinegar, Worcestershire, lime juice, salt and pepper.

4. Pour dressing over potato mixture and toss gently.

Makes 6 servings

"Even one kid going hungry in America is one too many.
How can we stand by when the reality is that there are more than 12 million
underfed children in the U.S.? We can make a difference."

LeANN RIMES

HOLIDAY FUDGE

PREPARATION TIME: 5 MINUTES

COOK TIME: 10 MINUTES

CHILL TIME: 2 HOURS

....

2 packages (11.5 ounces each) milk-chocolate chips

¼ cup butter or margarine (I Can't Believe It's Not Butter!® Spread)

1 can (14 ounces) sweetened condensed milk

1 tablespoon vanilla extract

1 cup chopped nuts, such as walnuts or pecans

1. In the top of a double boiler set over simmering water, melt chocolate chips and butter or margarine; stir until smooth.

2. Mix in condensed milk and vanilla and remove from heat.

3. Stir in nuts and pour into greased 8-inch baking dish.

4. Chill 2 hours, or until set. Cut into 2-inch squares.

Makes 16 pieces

"What we call the American Dream is founded in our
principles of self-government. Those principles stem from a value system
based on fundamental rights and responsibilities. None of these
can exist without education and a full stomach. In fact,
you cannot have a democracy when your people are hungry.
It is fundamental that we cure this problem."

WAYNE AND AMY ROGERS

WAYNE'S FISH DISH

PREPARATION TIME: 20 MINUTES

COOK TIME: 25 MINUTES

....

¼ cup butter or margarine (I Can't Believe It's Not Butter!® Spread)

1 pound medium shrimp, peeled and deveined

2 cups sliced mushrooms

1 Vidalia onion, sliced

2 cloves garlic, minced

¼ cup Chardonnay wine

1 whole red snapper or grouper (about 4 pounds), cleaned and scaled, head and tail left on

Salt and pepper, to taste

6 cups cooked rice (optional)

Lemon wedges (optional)

1. Preheat broiler. In a 12-inch skillet, over medium-high heat, melt butter or margarine. Add shrimp, mushrooms, onion and garlic and cook 8 minutes, stirring occasionally, until vegetables are tender and shrimp turn pink. Add wine and cook 1 minute more.

2. With knife parallel to cutting board, make a deep long cut down center of fish to form pocket. On greased rack in broiler pan, arrange fish and season with salt and pepper, if desired. Stuff fish with half of the shrimp mixture. Reserve remaining shrimp mixture. Broil 5 minutes. Turn fish and broil an additional 5 minutes.

3. Arrange remaining shrimp mixture around fish; broil 2 minutes, or until fish flakes easily.

4. Serve, if desired, with rice and lemon wedges.

Makes 4 servings

"The food stamp programs and school meal programs
have served us well in the past. They need to be
protected and made more accessible to the needy—especially
our little ones. These programs can work."

MICKEY AND JAN ROONEY

PREPARATION TIME: 10 MINUTES

CHILL TIME: 30 MINUTES

....

1 pound fresh bocconcini (mozzarella cheese balls) or regular mozzarella, cut into chunks

2 large tomatoes, cut into chunks

1 jar (7½ ounces) roasted red peppers, drained and coarsely chopped

½ cup balsamic vinaigrette dressing (Wish-Bone®)

¼ cup loosely packed fresh basil leaves, chopped

¼ teaspoon salt

⅛ teaspoon black pepper

1. In large bowl, combine all ingredients. Cover and refrigerate at least 30 minutes to allow flavors to blend.

2. Stir well before serving.

Makes 6 appetizer servings

"Childhood hunger in America is as much a paradox
as it is a tragedy. Why, in the wealthiest country in the world,
should hunger darken the lives and dreams of
12 million children and their families? I believe that when Americans
learn the facts and understand how their involvement can
make a difference, banishing childhood hunger will be a national,
local and personal priority."

MARTIN SHEEN

PREPARATION TIME: 10 MINUTES

COOK TIME: 40 MINUTES

....

2 tablespoons olive oil (Bertolli®)

3 medium carrots, sliced

3 ribs celery, sliced

1 cup lentils, picked through and rinsed

1 envelope onion soup mix (Lipton® Recipe Secrets®)

1 tablespoon cider vinegar or red-wine vinegar

4 cups hot cooked couscous, brown rice or pasta

1. In a 3-quart saucepan, heat oil over medium heat and cook carrots and celery, stirring occasionally, 3 minutes.

2. Add lentils and cook 1 minute. Stir in 2 cups water. Bring to a boil over high heat.

3. Reduce heat to low and simmer, covered, stirring occasionally, 25 minutes. Blend soup mix with 1 cup water and stir into lentil mixture.

4. Simmer, covered, an additional 10 minutes, or until lentils are tender. Stir in vinegar. Serve over hot couscous.

Makes 4 servings

"It's hard to believe that in the 1970s, America was virtually hunger-free. During the past two decades, we have allowed hunger to attack our most precious resource, our children. We must reinstate and strengthen programs to eliminate this blight on our society."

KURTWOOD SMITH

PREPARATION TIME: 5 MINUTES

COOK TIME: 5 TO 6 MINUTES

....

½ cup oatmeal (quick-cooking or old-fashioned)

½ small apple, chopped

1 cup skim milk

⅛ teaspoon ground cinnamon

¼ cup raisins

1 medium banana, sliced

¼ cup fresh berries

1 tablespoon chopped nuts

1. In large microwave-safe bowl, combine oatmeal, apple, milk and cinnamon.

2. Microwave on HIGH 2½ minutes. Stir in raisins and microwave on HIGH 1 minute. Stir in banana and microwave on HIGH 1 minute. Stir in berries and microwave on HIGH 1 minute more.

3. Stir in nuts and serve.

Makes 2 servings

Serving suggestion: Round out your breakfast with cups of hot Lipton® Tea.

"It has been a pleasure to join the many individuals
and organizations committed to ending hunger over the years.
During my tenure in the U.S. Senate, I have joined
with many of my colleagues to address this serious problem in our nation
and abroad. I am concerned by the evidence demonstrating that
inadequate nutrition can have a detrimental impact on children's ability
to learn in school and adults' level of functioning in the workplace.
As individuals, governments and a global community,
we have a responsibility to solve hunger and its consequences.
Working together, we have the opportunity to positively
affect people's lives and our collective future."

SENATOR ARLEN SPECTER

CARAMEL-PINEAPPLE CAKE ROLL

PREPARATION TIME: 20 MINUTES

COOK TIME: 18 TO 20 MINUTES

....

2 cans (8¼ ounces each) crushed pineapple, drained

½ cup dark brown sugar

¾ cup cake flour

1 teaspoon baking powder

½ teaspoon salt

4 eggs, separated

¾ cup granulated sugar

2 teaspoons vanilla extract

1 teaspoon grated lemon peel

6 tablespoons confectioners' sugar, divided

1 cup whipping or heavy cream

1. Preheat oven to 375°F. Evenly spread pineapple in bottom of a greased 15-inch-by-10-inch jelly-roll pan; sprinkle with brown sugar.

2. Sift flour with baking powder and salt; set aside.

3. In large bowl, with electric mixer at high speed, beat egg whites until foamy. Gradually add granulated sugar and beat until stiff.

4. In a separate bowl, beat egg yolks and vanilla at medium speed. Stir in lemon peel. Gently fold egg whites into this mixture, then fold eggs into flour mixture. Spread evenly over pineapple in pan.

5. Bake 18 to 20 minutes. Loosen edges of cake from pan with a butter knife and invert onto damp cloth towel. Sprinkle with 3 tablespoons confectioners' sugar. Roll cake up in towel and let cool.

6. Meanwhile, prepare frosting. In medium bowl, with electric mixer at high speed, beat cream and the remaining 3 tablespoons confectioners' sugar until stiff.

7. Remove towel from cooled cake and place on serving platter. Spread with frosting and serve.

Makes 8 servings

Serving suggestion: A fresh pot of Lipton® Tea is a satisfying accompaniment.

"A society is judged by the way it cares for its most vulnerable citizens. As an American, I am ashamed that we have turned our backs on millions of children. I want to do my part to rectify this terrible situation."

MARLO THOMAS

PREPARATION TIME: 25 MINUTES

CHILL TIME: 30 MINUTES

½ cup cracked wheat (bulgar)

2 bunches parsley

1 bunch mint, or 1 tablespoon dried mint leaves

2 bunches green onions (scallions), chopped (about 1 cup)

4 large tomatoes, chopped

½ cup fresh lemon juice (about 4 lemons)

Salt and pepper, to taste

Romaine lettuce leaves

½ cup olive oil (Bertolli®)

1. Place cracked wheat in bowl; fill with cold water to cover. Soak 15 minutes; drain, then squeeze dry in cloth towel.

2. Meanwhile, soak parsley and mint in salted water 5 minutes. Rinse well, then pat dry and chop.

3. In large bowl, combine cracked wheat, onions, tomatoes, parsley and mint. Stir in lemon juice and salt and pepper; chill at least 30 minutes.

4. To serve, arrange tabbouleh on lettuce leaves and drizzle with oil.

Makes 8 servings

Serving suggestion: Enjoy with Lipton® Onion Burgers. To make 8 servings, in a large bowl, combine 1 envelope Lipton® Recipe Secrets® Onion Soup Mix with 2 pounds ground beef. Add ½ cup water and mix well. Shape into 8 patties. Grill or broil until done. Serve with tomato slices and lettuce on hamburger buns.

"We don't think of the long-term damage that the persistence
of hunger could cause. Hungry children cannot reach their full potential.
Every child deserves that chance."

LEA THOMPSON

PREPARATION TIME: 10 MINUTES

STANDING TIME: 1 HOUR, 10 MINUTES

COOK TIME: 16 MINUTES

···

Mesquite charcoal

1½ teaspoons garlic salt (Lawry's®)

½ teaspoon salt

½ teaspoon black pepper

2- to 3-pound beef sirloin roast

1 cup oak or mesquite chips

1. Ninety minutes before serving, place charcoal in grill and light.

2. Meanwhile, in small bowl, combine garlic salt, salt and pepper; rub on beef. Cover; let stand at room temperature 1 hour.

3. Soak chips in water 30 minutes. Bank fire on either side of grill. Drain chips and add to fire. Place an aluminum foil pan in the middle.

4. Cover grill with vents open, for 2 minutes, to let smoke build up. Uncover and cook meat over fire, 2 to 3 minutes on each side.

5. Transfer meat to center section away from direct heat and cover grill. Let cook 5 minutes; turn roast, cover and cook 5 minutes more. Cook to desired doneness, using an instant-read thermometer.

6. Let meat stand 10 minutes on platter before slicing; cut across grain. Serve any juice over meat or baked potatoes.

Makes 8 to 12 servings

Serving suggestion: Serve with corn on the cob and a tomato salad topped with Wish-Bone® Balsamic Vinaigrette Dressing.

"The encouraging news about this problem is that we can solve it. Our country has all the resources we need to do it. We can all be part of the solution by getting involved. I pledge to help in any way I can."

CHERYL TIEGS

PREPARATION TIME: 5 MINUTES

CHILL TIME: 4 HOURS OR OVERNIGHT

COOK TIME: 30 MINUTES

···

1 cup low-sodium soy sauce

⅓ cup fresh lemon juice (about 3 lemons)

⅓ cup honey

¼ cup olive oil (Bertolli®)

¼ cup dry sherry

¼ cup Worcestershire sauce

1 to 3 teaspoons grated fresh ginger

4 pounds chicken drumsticks

1. In large bowl, combine all ingredients except chicken.
2. In large, shallow nonaluminum baking dish or plastic bag, combine chicken and marinade. Cover, or close bag, and marinate in refrigerator 4 hours or overnight.
3. Remove chicken from marinade; discard marinade. Grill or broil chicken, turning occasionally, 30 minutes, or until chicken is no longer pink.

Makes 12 servings

Serving suggestion: Lipton® Noodles & Sauce (Alfredo variety) makes a tasty side dish.

"Let's share our abundance and make our country stronger. We can encourage programs that collect and distribute excess prepared food to local organizations that are helping the hungry in our own communities. We can also support programs that supply commodities to food banks. It's all part of committing our country's wealth and resources to end childhood hunger."

JOHN TRAVOLTA

TUNA TARTARE WITH WON TON CRISPS

PREPARATION TIME: 15 MINUTES

CHILL TIME: 1 HOUR

COOK TIME: 10 MINUTES

....

5 ounces raw ahi tuna, diced

¼ cup diced cucumber

3 tablespoons diced avocado

1 tablespoon sesame oil

1 tablespoon fresh lime juice

1 tablespoon mayonnaise (Hellmann's® or Best Foods®)

¼ teaspoon chili oil

Salt and pepper, to taste

1 cup extra-light olive oil (Bertolli®)

4 refrigerated won ton skins (wrappers), each cut into 4 triangles, or tortilla chips

1. In large bowl, combine tuna, cucumber, avocado, sesame oil, lime juice, mayonnaise, chili oil and salt and pepper; chill about 1 hour.

2. Meanwhile, in a 12-inch skillet, heat olive oil over medium-high heat and fry skins in small batches until golden, turning once. Drain on paper towels and cool completely.

3. Serve tuna tartare with fried won ton crisps or tortilla chips.

Makes 4 appetizer servings

Serving suggestion: Enjoy with Lipton® Iced Tea.

"In this country that grows more food than any other nation on this earth, it is unthinkable that any child should go hungry."

SELA WARD

SELA'S HUMMINGBIRD CAKE

PREPARATION TIME: **15** MINUTES
COOK TIME: **25** MINUTES

....

3 cups all-purpose flour

2 cups sugar

1 teaspoon salt

1 teaspoon baking soda

1 teaspoon ground cinnamon

3 eggs, beaten

1½ cups vegetable oil

3½ teaspoons vanilla extract, divided

1 can (8 ounces) crushed pineapple, undrained

2 cups chopped bananas (about 4)

2 cups chopped pecans, divided

2 packages (8 ounces each) cream cheese, softened

1 cup butter or margarine (I Can't Believe It's Not Butter!® Spread)

2 boxes (16 ounces each) confectioners' sugar

Dash salt

1. Preheat oven to 350°F. In large bowl, combine flour, sugar, salt, baking soda and cinnamon. Add eggs and oil and stir until moistened.

2. Stir in 1½ teaspoons vanilla extract, pineapple, bananas and 1 cup chopped pecans.

3. Spoon batter into 3 greased and floured 9-inch cake pans.

4. Bake 25 minutes, or until toothpick inserted in centers of cakes come out clean. Cool in pans 10 minutes. Remove from pans and cool completely on wire racks.

5. Meanwhile, prepare frosting. In large bowl, with electric mixer at medium speed, beat cream cheese and butter or margarine until smooth. Add confectioners' sugar and beat until light and fluffy. Stir in the remaining 2 teaspoons vanilla and salt.

6. Generously spread frosting between cooled cake layers and on sides and top of cake. Garnish with the remaining 1 cup pecans.

Makes 8 servings

Serving suggestion: Accompany slices of this elegant cake with steaming cups of Lipton® Tea.

"There can be no lasting peace, no security, nor can we
as human beings begin to touch our full potential, as long as hunger
overwhelms the human spirit around this planet."

DENNIS WEAVER

JICAMA COOLER SALAD

PREPARATION TIME: 15 MINUTES

CHILL TIME: 30 MINUTES

....

1 large jicama, peeled

1 medium sweet onion, finely chopped

1 large cucumber, peeled, seeded and diced

1 medium tomato, peeled and diced

Ume plum vinegar or balsamic salad dressing (Wish-Bone®), to taste

1. Grate jicama and briefly drain in a colander or strainer.

2. In medium bowl, combine all ingredients; chill for 30 minutes to blend flavors before serving.

Makes 4 servings

Serving suggestion: Team up this refreshing side dish with a pitcher of Lipton® Iced Tea.

"We feel that no one, anywhere, should ever go hungry,
especially in a first-world nation where we have so many resources.
Food is something the earth gave us, and it should be free.
We could cultivate more organizations around the nation to feed hungry people.
It would be nice to see more small, organic farms as well."

CARNIE AND WENDY WILSON

SALMON A LA CHECCA

PREPARATION TIME: 20 MINUTES

COOK TIME: 15 MINUTES

....

¼ teaspoon garlic powder (Lawry's®)

¼ teaspoon onion powder

¼ teaspoon salt

¼ teaspoon black pepper

2 salmon fillets (about 6 ounces each)

1 tablespoon balsamic vinegar

3 tablespoons olive oil (Bertolli®), divided

Juice of 2 lemons, divided

4 medium tomatoes, cut into 1-inch pieces

2 large garlic cloves, finely chopped

4 large basil leaves, julienned

⅛ teaspoon cayenne pepper

Salt and pepper, to taste

1. Preheat oven to 375°F. In small bowl, mix garlic powder, onion powder, salt and pepper.
2. Place salmon in 13-inch-by-9-inch baking dish and coat with spice mixture.
3. In another small bowl, combine vinegar, 1 tablespoon oil and half the lemon juice; pour over salmon. Bake 15 minutes, or until salmon flakes easily with fork.
4. Meanwhile, in small bowl, combine tomatoes, garlic, basil, the remaining 2 tablespoons oil and lemon juice, cayenne and salt and pepper.
5. To serve, spoon tomato mixture over salmon.

Makes 2 servings

Serving suggestion: Enjoy with Lipton® Rice & Sauce (Pilaf variety) and hot Lipton® Tea.

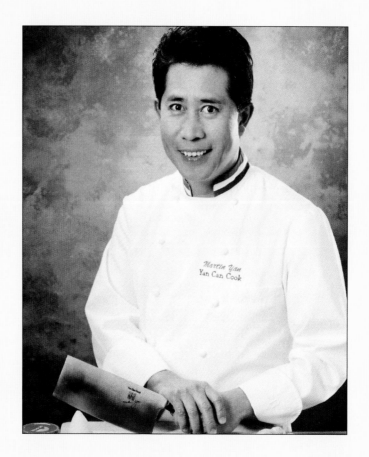

"Nobody can understand hunger unless they've experienced it.
I did as a child. The experience has given me a blessed appreciation for food
and nourishment. I am grateful that I no longer have to suffer
the pangs of hunger, but many children and adults in this world still do.
Whenever food is placed before you, enjoy and appreciate it.
And remember to help provide sustenance to those less fortunate.
No one should ever go to bed hungry."

CHEF MARTIN YAN

GRILLED CHICKEN SALAD

PREPARATION TIME: 20 MINUTES
CHILL TIME: 30 MINUTES
COOK TIME: 10 MINUTES

....

3 tablespoons soy sauce, divided

1 tablespoon sesame oil

⅛ teaspoon white pepper

1 boneless, skinless chicken breast (about 6 ounces)

¼ cup apple-cider vinegar

3 tablespoons chunky peanut butter (Skippy®)

2 tablespoons honey

1 teaspoon hot-pepper sauce

¼ cup olive oil (Bertolli®)

5 cups shredded iceberg lettuce

1 medium red bell pepper, halved, seeded and thinly sliced

½ cucumber, peeled, seeded and julienned

½ cup honey-glazed walnuts or peanuts

1. In small bowl or plastic bag, mix 2 tablespoons soy sauce, sesame oil and white pepper. Place chicken in bowl or bag. Cover or close bag, and marinate in refrigerator 30 minutes.

2. Remove chicken from marinade; discard marinade. Grill or broil chicken 10 minutes, or until no longer pink, turning once. Let cool slightly; cut into thin strips.

3. In small bowl, combine vinegar, peanut butter, honey, the remaining 1 tablespoon soy sauce and hot-pepper sauce. Gradually whisk in olive oil until smooth; set aside.

4. In large bowl, combine lettuce, bell pepper and cucumber.

5. To serve, toss lettuce mixture with dressing and arrange on serving platter. Top with chicken and nuts.

Makes 2 servings

Recipe created by Martin's wife, Susan Yoshimura

How many hungry families are there in your state, and where can you go to help them? Below is a listing of Hunger Free America State Coalition Leaders in each state and the District of Columbia, as well as some sobering—and motivating—statistics compiled by the Center on Hunger and Poverty at Brandeis University in Waltham, Massachusetts. The higher the number of a state's ranking, the higher the percentage of hungry and food insecure households within its borders. For more information visit *www.hungerfreeamerica.org*.

ALABAMA
Alabama Coalition Against Hunger
(334) 262-0359

11.3% of hungry and food insecure households
24.1% of children living in poverty
State ranking: 40

ALASKA
Food Bank of Alaska
(907) 272-3663
http://www.fba.ak.org

7.6% of hungry and food insecure households
10.7% of children living in poverty
State ranking: 13

ARIZONA
Association of Arizona Food Banks
(602) 528-3434
http://www.azfoodbanks.org

St. Mary's Food Bank
(602) 352-3640
http://www.smfb.org

12.8% of hungry and food insecure households
26.4% of children living in poverty
State ranking: 48 (tied with Louisiana)

ARKANSAS
Arkansas Hunger Coalition
(501) 374-6675, x501

12.6% of hungry and food insecure households
16.7% of children living in poverty
State ranking: 46 (tied with Oregon)

CALIFORNIA
California Food Policy Advocates
(415) 777-4422, x102
http://www.cfpa.net

California WIC Association
(916) 448-2280

11.4% of hungry and food insecure households
23.6% of children living in poverty
State ranking: 41

COLORADO
Food Bank of the Rockies
(303) 371-9250
http://foodbankrockies.org

8.8% of hungry and food insecure households
13.7% of children living in poverty
State ranking: 28 (tied with Connecticut, North Carolina, Utah)

CONNECTICUT
Connecticut Anti-Hunger Coalition
(860) 951-2212, x238

Connecticut Food Bank
(203) 469-5000
http://www.ctfoodbank.org

8.8% of hungry and food insecure households
12.1% of children living in poverty
State ranking: 28 (tied with Colorado, North Carolina, Utah)

DELAWARE
Food Bank of Delaware
(302) 292-1305, x214
http://www.fbd.org

6.8% of hungry and food insecure households
16.1% of children living in poverty
State ranking: 4

DISTRICT OF COLUMBIA
Greater Washington Food Bank
(202) 526-5344
http://www.washingtonpost.com/yp/food-bank

11.1% of hungry and food insecure households
45.3% of children living in poverty
State ranking: 39

FLORIDA
Florida Association of Community Action
(352) 378-6517
http://www.faca.org

11.5% of hungry and food insecure households

22.3% of children living in poverty
State ranking: 42

GEORGIA
Georgia Citizens' Coalition on Hunger
(404) 622-7778

9.7% of hungry and food insecure households
23.4% of children living in poverty
State ranking: 31

HAWAII
Hawaii Foodbank, Inc.
(808) 836-3600, x222

10.4% of hungry and food insecure households
15.1% of children living in poverty
State ranking: 37

IDAHO
Idaho Hunger Action Council
(206) 568-5400

10.1% of hungry and food insecure households
20.1% of children living in poverty
State ranking: 34

ILLINOIS
Chicago Anti-Hunger Federation
(773) 252-3663
http://www.anti-hunger.org

8.2% of hungry and food insecure households
13.8% of children living in poverty
State ranking: 17

INDIANA
Gleaners Food Bank of Indiana
(317) 925-0191, x111
http://www.gleaners.org

7.8% of hungry and food insecure households
12% of children living in poverty
State ranking: 15

IOWA
Foodbank of Iowa
(515) 564-0330

7% of hungry and food insecure households
15.5% of children living in poverty
State ranking: 6

KANSAS
Campaign to End Childhood Hunger in Kansas
(316) 264-9303

9.9% of hungry and food insecure households
12.9% of children living in poverty
State ranking: 32

KENTUCKY
Kentucky Task Force on Hunger
(859) 266-2521

8.4% of hungry and food insecure households
18.6% of children living in poverty
State ranking: 19

LOUISIANA
Greater Baton Rouge Food Bank
(225) 359-9940
http://www.brfoodbank.org

12.8% of hungry and food insecure households
29.2% of children living in poverty
State ranking: 48 (tied with Arizona)

MAINE
Maine Coalition for Food Security
(207) 871-8266
http://www.mefoodsecurity.org

Partners in Ending Hunger
(207) 236-9643
http://www.endhungernow.org

8.7% of hungry and food insecure households
14.3% of children living in poverty
State ranking: 24 (tied with Rhode Island)

MARYLAND
Center for Poverty Solutions
(401) 366-0600, x108
http://www.ctrforpovertysolutions.org

7.1% of hungry and food insecure households
7.5% of children living in poverty
State ranking: 8 (tied with Pennsylvania)

MASSACHUSETTS
Springfield College
(413) 748-3354
http://www.spfldcol.edu

Project Bread/The Walk for Hunger
(617) 723-5000
http://www.projectbread.org

6.3% of hungry and food insecure households
13.8% of children living in poverty
State ranking: 2

MICHIGAN
Hunger Action Coalition of Michigan
(313) 963-7788, x28
http://comnet.org/hacmi

8.1% of hungry and food insecure households
15.6% of children living in poverty
State ranking: 16

MINNESOTA
Urban Coalition/Hunger and Poverty Office
(612) 348-8550, x226
http://www.urbancoalition.org

Minnesota Food Share
(612) 721-8687
http://www.gmcc.org/MFS/

6.9% of hungry and food insecure households
15.4% of children living in poverty
State ranking: 5

MISSISSIPPI
Mississippi Food Network
(601) 353-6656

14% of hungry and food insecure households
21.8% of children living in poverty
State ranking: 50

MISSOURI
Food Bank Association of Missouri
(573) 474-1020

8.6% of hungry and food insecure households
15.6% of children living in poverty
State ranking: 22 (tied with Nevada)

MONTANA
Montana Hunger Coalition
(406) 327-9201

10.2% of hungry and food insecure households
22.6% of children living in poverty
State ranking: 36 (tied with South Carolina)

NEBRASKA
The Nebraska Food Bank Network
(402) 331-1213

7.5% of hungry and food insecure households

16.2% of children living in poverty
State ranking: 12

NEVADA
Food Bank of Northern Nevada
(775) 331-3663
http://www.fbnn.org

8.6% of hungry and food insecure households
13.7% of children living in poverty
State ranking: 22 (tied with Missouri)

NEW HAMPSHIRE
New Hampshire Food Bank
(603) 669-9725

7.4% of hungry and food insecure households
14.7% of children living in poverty
State ranking: 11

NEW JERSEY
Center for Food Action in New Jersey
(201) 569-1804, x23

7.3% of hungry and food insecure households
12.2% of children living in poverty
State ranking: 10

NEW MEXICO
New Mexico Association of Food Banks
(505) 247-2052

15.1% of hungry and food insecure households
26.3% of children living in poverty
State ranking: 51

NEW YORK
Nutrition Consortium of New York State
(518) 436-8757, x15
ncnys@crisny.org

10% of hungry and food insecure households
24.6% of children living in poverty
State ranking: 33

NORTH CAROLINA
North Carolina Hunger Network
(919) 821-5300

8.8% of hungry and food insecure households
21.5% of children living in poverty
State ranking: 28 (tied with Colorado, Connecticut, Utah)

NORTH DAKOTA
Great Plains Food Bank
(701) 232-6219
http://www.lssnd.org/program16.html

4.6% of hungry and food insecure
households
20.6% of children living in poverty
State ranking: 1

OHIO
Ohio Hunger Task Force
(614) 341-7700
http://www.ohtf.org

Ohio Food Policy Action Center
(614) 759-9215

Ohio Association Of Second Harvest
Food Banks
(614) 221-4336
http://www.secondharvest.org

8.5% of hungry and food insecure
households
18% of children living in poverty
State ranking: 20

OKLAHOMA
Regional Food Bank of Oklahoma
(405) 972-1111, x117
http://www.regionalfoodbank.org

11.9% of hungry and food insecure
households
19.5% of children living in poverty
State ranking: 44 (tied with
Washington)

OREGON
Oregon Hunger Relief Task Force
(503) 963-2290
http://www.hcs.state.or.us

12.6% of hungry and food insecure
households
21.6% of children living in poverty
State ranking: 46 (tied with Arkansas)

PENNSYLVANIA
Pennsylvania Hunger Coalition
(717) 233-6705

7.1% of hungry and food insecure
households
18.2% of children living in poverty
State ranking: 8 (tied with Maryland)

RHODE ISLAND
Rhode Island Community Food Bank
(410) 826-3073, x216
http://www.rifoodbank.org

8.7% of hungry and food insecure
households

19.4% of children living in poverty
State ranking: 24 (tied with Maine)

SOUTH CAROLINA
South Carolina Committee Against
Hunger
(843) 792-7270

10.2% of hungry and food insecure
households
18.1% of children living in poverty
State ranking: 36 (tied with Montana)

SOUTH DAKOTA
Black Hills Regional Second Harvest
Food Bank
(605) 348-2689

Food Service Center of South Dakota
(605) 335-0364

6.4% of hungry and food insecure
households
11.7% of children living in poverty
State ranking: 3

TENNESSEE
Tennessee Hunger Coalition
(423) 434-0270

10.9% of hungry and food insecure
households
18.1% of children living in poverty
State ranking: 38

TEXAS
Texas Anti-Hunger Network
(512) 320-0222

Texas Alliance for Human Needs
(512) 474-5019
http://www.txalliance.org

12.9% of hungry and food insecure
households
22% of children living in poverty
State ranking: 49

UTAH
Utahns Against Hunger
(801) 328-2561

8.8% of hungry and food insecure
households
14% of children living in poverty
State ranking: 28 (tied with Colorado,
Connecticut, North Carolina)

VERMONT
Vermont Campaign to End Childhood
Hunger
(802) 865-0255

7.7% of hungry and food insecure
households
14.3% of children living in poverty
State ranking: 14

VIRGINIA
Virginia's Table/Central Virginia
Foodbank Inc.
(804) 521-2500

Virginia Council Against Poverty
(804) 644-0417

8.3% of hungry and food insecure
households
9% of children living in poverty
State ranking: 18

WASHINGTON
Children's Alliance
(509) 747-7205
http://www.childrensalliance.org

11.9% of hungry and food insecure
households
11.2% of children living in poverty
State ranking: 44 (tied with Oklahoma)

WEST VIRGINIA
West Virginia Coalition on Food and
Nutrition
(304) 342-9120

9% of hungry and food insecure households
27.5% of children living in poverty
State ranking: 30 (tied with Wyoming)

WISCONSIN
Hunger Task Force of Milwaukee
(414) 777-0483
http://www.hungertaskforce.org

7.2% of hungry and food insecure
households
13.5% of children living in poverty
State ranking: 9

WYOMING
Wyoming Hunger Coalition/NOWCAP
(307) 347-3976
http://www.trib.com/nowcap

9% of hungry and food insecure households
14.9% of children living in poverty
State ranking: 30 (tied with Wisconsin)

Statistics compiled by the Center on Hunger and Poverty, Brandeis University from the following sources: M.Nord et al (September 1999) *Prevalence of Food Insecurity and Hunger, by State, 1996-98*. Washington, DC: Economic Research Service, USDA, and its Addendum, *How Many Households? How Many People?* (August 2000). Child poverty figures based upon government data. All hunger and food insecurity statistics are based on averages for the years 1996-1998.

Buzz Aldrin   Edward Asner   Neil and Lisa Beckerman

Ed Begley Jr.   Edward James Olmos   The Bellamy Brothers

Lesley Boone   The Bridges Family   Beau Bridges   Christie Brinkley

Erin Brockovich   Pierce and Keely Brosnan   Cheryl Chase

Chef Leah Chase   Katie Couric

Ted Danson and Mary Steenburgen   Kristen Davis   Bruce Davison

Bo Derek   Hector Elizondo   Dennis Franz

Scott and Carol Glenn   Linda Gray   Steve Guttenberg   Edie Hand

Mariel Hemingway   Don Henley   Catherine Hicks

Elizabeth Hurley   Kathy Ireland   Beverly Johnson   Senator Edward M. Kennedy

Graham Kerr   Swoosie Kurtz   Diane Ladd

Martin Landau   Jay Leno   Kenny Loggins   Joan Lunden

Pamela Sue Martin   Tim McGraw   Donna Mills

Kevin Nealon   Craig T. Nelson   Donny Osmond   Dolly Parton

Alexandra Paul   Chef Pepin   Bonnie Raitt

LeAnn Rimes   Wayne and Amy Rogers

Mickey and Jan Rooney   Martin Sheen   Kurtwood Smith

Senator Arlen Specter   Marlo Thomas   Lea Thompson   Cheryl Tiegs

John Travolta   Sela Ward   Dennis Weaver

Carnie and Wendy Wilson   Chef Martin Yan

Buzz Aldrin   Edward Asner   Neil and Lisa Beckerman

Ed Begley Jr.   Edward James Olmos   The Bellamy Brothers

Lesley Boone   The Bridges Family   Beau Bridges   Christie Brinkley

Erin Brockovich   Pierce and Keely Brosnan   Cheryl Chase

Chef Leah Chase   Katie Couric

Ted Danson and Mary Steenburgen   Kristen Davis   Bruce Davison

Bo Derek   Hector Elizondo   Dennis Franz

Scott and Carol Glenn   Linda Gray   Steve Guttenberg   Edie Hand

Mariel Hemingway   Don Henley   Catherine Hicks

Elizabeth Hurley   Kathy Ireland   Beverly Johnson   Senator Edward M. Kennedy

Graham Kerr   Swoosie Kurtz   Diane Ladd

Martin Landau   Jay Leno   Kenny Loggins   Joan Lunden

Pamela Sue Martin   Tim McGraw   Donna Mills

Kevin Nealon   Craig T. Nelson   Donny Osmond   Dolly Parton

Alexandra Paul   Chef Pepin   Bonnie Raitt

LeAnn Rimes   Wayne and Amy Rogers

Mickey and Jan Rooney   Martin Sheen   Kurtwood Smith

Senator Arlen Specter   Marlo Thomas   Lea Thompson   Cheryl Tiegs

John Travolta   Sela Ward   Dennis Weaver

Carnie and Wendy Wilson   Chef Martin Yan